How to inspire
and develop
positive values in
your classroom

Neil Hawkes

How to inspire and develop positive values in your classroom
LL01715
ISBN 1 85503 371 2
© Neil Hawkes
Illustrations by Rebecca Barnes
All rights reserved
First published 2003
Reprinted 2003 (twice)

The right of Neil Hawkes to be identified as the author of this work has been asserted by him in accordance with sections 77 and 78 of the Copyright, Designs and Patents Act 1988.

Printed in the UK for LDA
Duke Street, Wisbech, Cambs, PE13 2AE UK
3195 Wilson Drive NW, Grand Rapids, MI 49544 USA

Contents

Acknowledgements

It would have been impossible for this book to be written without the active support and inspiration of many teachers. As headteacher (1993–1999) of West Kidlington Primary and Nursery School in Oxfordshire, I worked with an outstanding group of teachers, non-teaching staff, governors and parents who gave me 100 per cent of their support as we developed values education in the school. It is impossible to express the gratitude I owe to West Kidlington School's community.

I am similarly indebted to the members of the Oxfordshire values task team for their dedicated hard work over the last three years. Much of the thinking in this book is drawn from their work and experience. They are Bridget Knight, Lindsey Weimers, Marilyn Trigg, Karen Errington, Linda Heppenstall, Alison Williams, Lucy Wilson, Peter Williams, Anne Marks, Louise McGinty, Nadine Vaillant-Hill and John Heppenstall. Also, my gratitude to the teachers at Stonesfield and Windmill primary schools whose work is featured in this book. Thanks too to Richard Howard and my colleagues in the Education Department at Oxford for supporting the development of values education in Oxfordshire.

A very special word of thanks to Frances Farrer, the author of *A Quiet Revolution*, the acclaimed book about the development of values education at West Kidlington School (see page 59). Frances's enthusiasm and desire to understand the methods used at the school enabled me to refine my thinking in preparation for the writing of this book for teachers.

Sincere thanks for the inspiration and support of many teachers around the world who are part of the UNICEF-sponsored programme Living Values. I am delighted to commend the resource materials contained in Education in Human Values, the Human Values Foundation's education programme. I am also indebted to Rose Kelly for being a brilliant sounding-board and making suggestions that have improved the text. And thanks to Corin Redsell, the book's editor, whose vision and enthusiasm encouraged me to write it.

Finally, thanks to my wonderful family and friends for their loving support.

Neil Hawkes

Preface

Thank you for reading *How to inspire and develop positive values in your classroom*. I believe that it can be an invaluable tool to help you introduce and develop values education, either as a class teacher with your particular class, or as a headteacher in the whole of your school.

The purpose of values education is as follows:
- To help your class and school community think about and reflect upon positive universal values and the practical implications of expressing them in relation to themselves, others, the community and the world.
- To inspire individuals to choose their own positive personal, social, moral and spiritual values and be aware of ways of developing and deepening them as citizens of the world.

'Values education encourages pupils to take greater responsibility for their behaviour and learning.'

I am convinced that values education supports teachers in promoting both an inclusive school ethos and methods of working that raise achievement. It helps pupils to develop their emotional literacy by improving their self-esteem. Teachers tell me that values education encourages their pupils to take greater responsibility for their behaviour and learning. Overall, it enables them to think about the kind of life that is worth living and to consider what kind of life they want for themselves.

At the core of values education lies the establishment of an agreed set of principles, deeply held convictions, that underpin all aspects of a school's life and work. The process is holistic and developmental, demanding a great deal from you, whether headteacher or class teacher, and from the school's community. It is not a soft option. The initial demands made on you and the school or class have a tremendous return in terms of improved ethos, relationships, pupil behaviour, quality of work and general achievement. Teachers tell me that once the system is embedded, their work becomes easier. This is a great selling point for values education.

During recent years a great deal of national and local effort has been directed at school improvement and curriculum development. Despite extensive innovation, many schools report that pupil attitudes and behaviour are all too often negative and challenging. Such behaviour inhibits the development of a school ethos that raises achievement and encourages pupils to be self-disciplined and to develop holistically. Research, such as undertaken by Hay McBer into school effectiveness, indicates that it is the degree to which a school can develop a positive school climate that is the main prerequisite for success.

In Frances Farrer's book about values education at West Kidlington School in Oxfordshire, I talked about my experience as a trainee teacher. On final teaching practice, which lasted for a whole term, I worked with an inspirational teacher called Peter Long at a village school in Oxfordshire. I was much influenced by this brilliant teacher because of all the personal qualities that he

'The effective teacher acts as a role model for pupils.'

brought to his work with children. He had the highest expectations of himself and worked to be a model of good practice. The ethos of the school was calm, happy and purposeful. He had a full range of teaching skills, which included a sincere interest in others, the ability to listen attentively to children and natural respect for others. I watched the influence that he had on pupils and realised that the effective teacher acts as a role model for pupils – a daunting prospect! I went on to be a primary school teacher in Wiltshire, where I was able to develop my skills. I have always liked the company of children and over the next few years I worked to develop a classroom climate that supported the holistic development of my pupils. I found that I could develop good relationships with the most challenging of children. I discovered that the key to this was treating children with respect, never talking down to them. I learned to tell off the negative behaviour rather than the child, to listen carefully and to respond appropriately. Yes, there were challenging moments, because none of us is a saint! But making mistakes and learning from them is another key to personal development and an important one to share with pupils. The ability to say 'I'm sorry' has always been important to me. Other teachers continued to teach me – such as David Evans, who taught me the value of laughter and fun, essential ingredients in any classroom.

During the last ten years I have been working with teachers to develop a vision for school effectiveness based on values education that will inspire a school's community. Such inspiration acts as the mortar, the curriculum being the bricks in the wall of good practice. This book aims to assist you as you strive to do your very best for the children in your class or school.

I have written the book with the intention that it will be of practical support to you as you develop a values-based approach to teaching and learning. I am very much aware that an increasing number of schools are discovering the success of using such a rationale to underpin the curriculum. In recent months, I have been asked by many teachers to put together a helpful book that will act both as checklist and ideas bank for values education.

Citizenship is currently high on the educational agenda. The vision of a values-based school contained in this book will support your development of active citizenship. Values-based education is not a new subject to be incorporated into the curriculum; rather it is an educational philosophy, an approach to teaching and learning that underpins the way a class or school organises itself, develops relationships and promotes positive human values. Teachers who adopt such an approach report that there is a qualitative improvement in pupil attitudes and behaviour. Furthermore, test results are seen to improve and there is the added bonus of teachers finding that their work is less stressful and more fun.

I do hope that you enjoy reading the book and will adapt the ideas to suit the particular needs of your own pupils. My very warmest good wishes to you in doing that.

Chapter 1
Why introduce values education?

Values education opens up a pathway to further discussion. It provides a means for children to talk in depth about feelings and the wider world.

Anna Fairhurst, Year 4/5 teacher

Teachers are champions!

Are you a champion? The answer is a resounding yes! This is because you, like thousands of other teachers, are aware of a fundamental gap in the education system. Increasingly, children come to school with little understanding about values such as respect, peace, humility, co-operation, care, responsibility and honesty. It is you, the teacher, who is taking on more and more responsibility to enable children to think about and understand values and apply them in their lives.

What are values?

Why do we behave in the way we do? What is it that drives us to give to charity or to help children to develop as happy, stable people?

It is our values that determine our thinking and behaviour. They are the principles, fundamental convictions, standards or life stances that act as the general guides to our behaviour. They are enduring beliefs about what is worthwhile, the ideals for which we strive. They are the standards by which particular beliefs and actions are judged to be good or desirable. They help us to make decisions and evaluate the actions of others.

Here is a list of twelve values, used in the international Living Values programme. You can find out more about this programme by visiting its website; see page 59. On the next page there are some helpful definitions of the values; these are adapted from the Living Values posters.

Twelve values and their definitions

Co-operation

- Co-operation is helping one another.
- Co-operation is working together with patience.
- Co-operation is collective effort to reach a goal.

Happiness

- Happiness is love and peace inside.
- Happiness is knowing I am loved.
- Happiness is giving everyone good wishes.

Responsibility

- Responsibility is being fair.
- Responsibility is doing my share of the work.
- Responsibility is taking care of myself and others.

Simplicity

- Simplicity is appreciating the small things in life.
- Simplicity is natural and beautiful.
- Simplicity is no unnecessary thinking.

Freedom

- Freedom is choice.
- Freedom is living with dignity.
- Freedom is when rights are balanced with responsibilities.

Unity

- Unity is togetherness.
- Unity is collective strength and harmony.
- Unity is personal commitment.

Peace

- Peace is when we get along.
- Peace is having positive thoughts for myself and others.
- Peace begins within each one of us.

Respect

- Respect is knowing I am unique and valuable.
- Respect is liking who I am.
- Respect is listening to others.

Love

- Love is caring and sharing.
- Love is feeling safe.
- Love is wanting the best for all.

Tolerance

- Tolerance is accepting myself and others.
- Tolerance is knowing we are all different.
- Tolerance is being understanding and open minded.

Honesty

- Honesty is telling the truth.
- Honesty is trust.
- Honesty is being true to yourself and to others.

Humility

- Humility is self-respect and self-esteem.
- Humility is accepting everyone.
- Humility is courage and confidence.

What is values education?

Values education occurs when a class or, ideally, a whole school deliberately and systematically supports its curriculum with a set of universal positive values. The values are woven into the curriculum in order to give a variety of opportunities for them to be thought about and used in the life of the school, the community and wider society.

What is the relevance of values education?

Values education has the potential to support the development of peace and harmony throughout the world, by promoting a set of universally accepted values in schools.

The aim of values education is to promote a common ethic, a new paradigm, which supports the individual in developing a personal ethic, a moral attitude that will positively affect behaviour and contribute to the peace and wellbeing of society. Ideally, this process will lead to a global ethic that will encourage a radical change in the hearts of people. The intention is not to dilute distinctive cultural or religious identities but to further the search for a fundamental consensus based on shared values. The basis of these values is the Golden Rule (forms of which can be found in all the major world faiths and in ancient philosophies) that what you wish done to yourself you should do to others. Such an ethic potentially leads to the fundamental ideal that every human being should be treated humanely.

Why is values education needed?

Since the National Curriculum was introduced in 1988, teachers have felt that there has been little opportunity to discuss ethical and moral issues with children so that they can think about the sort of people that they wish to be. There is a growing recognition by teachers that children need to be given the opportunity to understand that they have a choice in the way that they behave. There is now an opportunity during personal, social and health education (PSHE) and citizenship lessons for teachers and pupils to explore values together. I am sure that few teachers would require convincing of the need. During recent years there have been many horrific events. Some were carried out by children and young people – such as the murders of James Bulger and of London headteacher Philip Lawrence; others were by adults – notably the mass murder of children and their teacher in Dunblane and the machete attack in a Walsall infant school. These and many other happenings have stirred the nation's conscience and created panic about morals.

All this has led to an increased recognition that in the educational system there is a lack of focus on personal and social development. UNESCO's Delors Report, *Learning: the Treasure Within*, states that the fundamental role of education is in personal and social development and that there is a necessity to build the ability in children to operate within positive universal values. This report invigorated the debate on the future of education. UNESCO strongly believes in education as a means of creating peace and international

'Values education has the potential to support the development of peace and harmony throughout the world.'

understanding, maintaining that people of the world must 'learn to be' and 'learn to live together'.

In responding to this awareness, many schools are adopting policies for the development of values education. That is the starting point that leads to a qualitative shift in the way the school works, in terms of both its curriculum and its relationships. Here is the experience of Bridget Knight, of Stonesfield School in Oxfordshire, who has enthusiastically embraced the introduction of values education.

I first came to know about values-based education when I was teaching at a school near West Kidlington, where Neil Hawkes was head. I was able to watch one of his assemblies and felt that there was something in what he was doing that 'spoke to me'. Therefore, when I took up my first headship post at Stonesfield Primary School it was one of the things I wanted to try to put into practice for myself, to see if I too could make it work.

Three years and a lot of hard work later, I feel that values education has become the cornerstone of our school. A parent recently commented, 'There's something about this school now'. It informs the way that we behave towards one another and guides our thinking. As I reflect on the past three years, I can see that there has been a certain methodology in my introduction of values education. I would say at the outset, however, that it all needs time to 'grow' and develop, and that children and staff need to be able to see and feel its influence all around them in everything they do, at all moments, for it to be authentic and valuable. As a staff we worked together to produce a policy statement that is written in our prospectus. This statement is the basis of the rationale in the model school policy on pages 56 to 57.

This chapter is headed with the question 'Why introduce values education?' Ten years of experience with teachers who embrace values education has shown me that it has the potential to help children to be happy, to live life to the full and to grow into caring and civilised adults. It helps to create a calm and peaceful climate in the classroom, where there is mutual respect. In other words, it supports the development of a good learning environment. It supports the development of emotional literacy as it positively affects self-confidence and self-esteem. It helps raise achievement. It helps pupils to appreciate difference in others and to appreciate themselves more.

Here is what Maddy, a Year 6 pupil, said about values education:
> I think the world was made as a family but it's all breaking up into
> different parts, yet with values education in our school now, we're
> learning how to behave as a family and to remember the world is a
> family. It's important for life skills. When I sit in assembly it's very
> peaceful and it makes me feel _me_ and think of my own ambitions. It gives
> me time to think things over and shows me the real _me_. It's like a door
> opening and showing you the way.

The following chapters will help you to introduce and develop values education in your school or classroom.

Chapter 2
Can you be a positive role model?

I sometimes find myself thinking, am I a very good model, do I try hard enough?
Jilly Johnston, Reception/Year 1 teacher

What is a role model?

Modern media, especially TV and magazines, often leave us feeling inadequate. We are presented with images of the ideal woman or man. These are unrealistic. Being a role model simply means behaving in the way in which you would like your pupils to behave. You are showing, by your own behaviour, what you expect of them. This is potentially a very effective way of building a positive climate and good relationships in your class. However, here is a word of warning. Be real and true to yourself. Your pupils will be quick to spot behaviour that is inconsistent with the real you, so don't pretend to be what you're not.

Why be a role model?

Take a moment's thought, and you will be able to give examples of people who are not good, positive role models. The footballer who is acting aggressively, the pop star who's into drugs, the soap star whose private life is a disaster zone – these are negative role models that pupils are often encouraged to copy. The result may be negative behaviour from the pupil. The influence of the media in making idols out of people with many problems is confusing. You cannot replace these people, but you can offer a positive alternative.

Research shows that the behaviour of the teacher is the most important factor in creating the climate for success or failure for the pupil. Take a look at the diagram on the next page of the relationship between teacher and pupil.

The central importance of the relationship between teacher and pupil

In the diagram, which is an integral part of Oxfordshire's curriculum vision statement, at the centre of the process of teaching and learning is a dialogue between the teacher and the pupil. Their behaviour is determined by the subtle interaction of their thoughts, feelings and values. Their personal qualities, their values, influence their relationship. When coupled with the teacher's enthusiasm, professional skills, knowledge and understanding, that relationship ensures that the pupil is well educated. The care, nurture and valuing of both pupil and teacher are vital for the wellbeing and success of the school.

"There's no need to shout!"

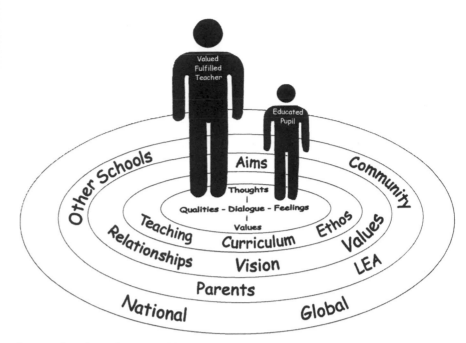

The pupil and teacher are affected by what the school does (curriculum) and how it does it (teaching). These build a climate for learning (ethos).

The interaction of curriculum, teaching and ethos forms the context for teaching and learning. This context emanates too from the school's vision (how it will educate the pupil). The vision is built on values (principles that influence behaviour), aims (what the school intends to do) and relationships (how everyone gets on). The school's vision is determined by parents, its community, other schools and the local education authority (LEA). These reflect both national and global influences. The outcome of this complex process, when successfully applied, is an educated, happy, civilised pupil and a professionally fulfilled teacher.

So now you can see why modelling values is significant. It is the single most important feature of the relationship between teacher and pupil. Your state of being is more influential than your state of doing.

I was recently visiting a London school in a socially challenging area. Behaviour was excellent and pupils were achieving in all aspects of the curriculum. The headteacher asked 10-year-old Tim to show me round the school. I asked him why everyone in the school behaved well. Here is his answer:

> *It's because we respect the teachers because they respect us. We have fun. We like the teachers. [I asked, 'Why do you like them?'] Because they're nice to us. They help us. If we get something wrong they don't put us down, they actually help us. Instead of taking the mick they help us to get it right instead. [I asked, 'What stops you playing up?'] It's respect because they're helping us and are on our side.*

In this school the teachers' state of being could be described as relaxed, happy and fulfilled. I asked one why they were like this. She replied, 'It's because we all feel valued and work happily together as a team.' There is no doubt that teaching in this atmosphere is easier and more rewarding.

How can you model values?

You can't model values that you don't think you have. I encourage you to give yourself space and time to let the values re-emerge in yourself. I believe that people have positive values and qualities within them but, unfortunately, the experiences that we have create a shield that stops them coming to the surface. By working on ourselves we allow them to show themselves in our attitudes and behaviour.

Making space and time to look within may appear scary. You may not be used to thinking about yourself or observing your own actions as a detached observer. Don't worry; relax, have a go. Some may find this difficult at first, but I promise it gets easier with practice.

To be confident as a role model requires effort. Here are some helpful tips:

- Get to know yourself and who you are. The better you know yourself and how you are seen by others, the more effective a role model you will be.
- Decide what qualities you wish to model. These may include *respect, patience, humour, caring, humility, simplicity, tolerance, honesty, peace* and *friendship*.
- Take each quality in turn and think about what it means. The twelve definitions in Chapter 1 may help. If you can, discuss them with others so that you build up an appreciation of these qualities.
- When you wake in the morning decide on one value that you are going to think about and model during the day. If it is *respect*, then as you interact with others during the day be conscious that you are treating them with respect. You will find that, after a while, working with the value becomes second nature and you don't have to think about it any more.
- Remember that these qualities you are focusing on are part of your original self and that you have simply forgotten them.
- A word of warning – don't berate yourself if your behaviour doesn't live up to your expectations. One sign of this is hearing a small voice that tells you off – it's your conscience. Another sign is playing the event that went wrong over and over again like a film. If you experience either of these, acknowledge the situation, remodel it in a more positive frame and replace the negative thought with the new one.
- At the end of the day review your progress, remembering to be patient yet determined. Next day continue the process.
- As you practise the values, you will find that change begins to happen. You will notice that others may respond to you slightly differently as they sense your change of attitude. It is true that what you give out you get back. Your positive attitude will bring its rewards.

Why is being a role model important?

The teacher is a model for the pupils in the classroom. Pupils copy their attitudes and behaviour. It is therefore important for the teacher to consider how they sit, their tone of voice, the degree to which they are authentic in their interactions with pupils. The ability of staff to model expected pupil

'The better you know yourself and how you are seen by others, the more effective a role model you will be.'

behaviour is key to the development of positive behaviour and to the raising of achievement. For instance, there is little point in talking about the value of respect if staff experience difficulty in respecting pupils. Chapter 3 gives practical suggestions about how values can be introduced into the classroom.

A teacher acting as a role model

In the following account, Linda, a teacher of 10-year-olds at West Kidlington Primary School, describes how she teaches values across the curriculum. She takes regular opportunities to encourage the children to reflect on their

Case study: Linda

One of my key skills as a teacher of values is my ability to use situations that arise naturally in my class as opportunities for pupils to consider the effects of their behaviour. I do this deliberately and systematically. As a result, the children start to question themselves about what they are doing and to look at things in a different light. They start to become responsible for what they are doing; they see what they are doing and why they are doing it. They look at it in terms of if it is right or wrong.

Let me give you some examples. At one time in my class some children were calling a boy racist names. They were unaware of just how much that hurt him. Their behaviour was the result of previous negative conditioning. To address this inappropriate behaviour I taught a lesson on the fact that everyone is different and has different talents and capabilities. I helped the pupils to understand that we are all the same inside, with the capacity to feel joy, happiness, fear and pain. It was only after the class had reflected on this and talked about it that they realised that their behaviour had been hurtful.

Another example was in a games lesson, when I was teaching rounders for the first time. Afterwards I sat the children down and told them how much I had disliked the session and why. During the lesson a boy had missed hitting the ball and someone had laughed. Later, when one child had been 'got out', someone else had laughed. Then one boy had been called out and went off. I heard him saying to someone 'Did you see what she did with the ball?' (I was bowling.)

At that point I decided to finish the lesson. I went through everything that happened, explaining why I disliked it. I asked them to think about how it made other people feel when you laughed at them and said that a games session should be about enjoying the game and helping and supporting each other. When they had games, I wanted everyone to enjoy it, including myself. If this could not happen, we would not play games. I then spoke individually to the people who had criticised, saying that I wanted them to think about what they had learnt and decide how they were going to behave the next time they played.

The children were positive at the end of the session. I was helping them to be reflective about their behaviour throughout their lives. That helps them to be more aware of what they are saying and doing at a particular moment. Incidentally, the next week we had a brilliant session.

behaviour. What you will sense in her account is that she is modelling positive behaviour through her own remarks, attitudes and expectations.

The two main ingredients in being a role model are modelling the desired behaviour and helping the pupils to reflect on their own behaviour.

Sometimes we are not aware of the values that we are modelling by our behaviour in class. On the next page there is a self-assessment checklist that will help you to look at yourself.

Modelling values
Some self-assessment questions

◗ Am I aware of the values that I convey to the pupils?

◗ What values do I model in the way I teach — patience and respect, for instance?

◗ Am I consistent in the messages (given in my words and actions) that I give to pupils during lessons and about the school?

◗ Am I calm and friendly?

◗ Am I prepared to share my own thoughts and experiences with pupils?

How can I informally model a values approach to parents?

Besides modelling values to pupils, you may wonder how you can model the values to parents and the wider community. My experience is that teachers who live their values don't think about modelling values because they themselves represent the values.

Here are some things to reflect on about your relationships with your pupils' parents or carers:

◗ Are you real, yourself and authentic when you are talking with parents?

◗ Are you warm and friendly to parents?

◗ Do you listen to parents carefully before giving replies to their questions?

◗ Are you able to be calm and reflective when they are emotionally wound up?

◗ Do you send notes home that are direct and informative, and that use the language of an equal partner?

◗ Do you make yourself available for informal discussions?

◗ Do you actively support parent/teacher social events?

If your answer to most of the questions above is yes, then you are modelling a values approach to parents. This is what Jilly Johnston thinks about role modelling:

> I sometimes find myself thinking: am I a very good role model, do I try hard enough? I am not sure if I think this because of the values at school or because I already hope that I follow them. I think that my childhood gave me a very good grounding to work on. I suppose I strive to make each day as meaningful, enjoyable and hopefully as exciting a time as I can. I am not saying that I get there every day but I try. Talking to children about values makes me think about my own values and constantly reminds me that perhaps I ought to try a bit harder. I think that you cannot expect children to be polite to you if you are not polite to them.

In the next chapter we think about how to make a start with values-based education.

Chapter 3
How you can introduce a values-based curriculum in your classroom

'Values education will bring tremendous benefits to the climate of your classroom.'

Values education gives a consistent approach to moral education. Nothing we do is piecemeal. We work on a two-year cycle and so there is continuity and progression as we reinforce and build on the work of our colleagues over the year. It creates a team spirit and is successful because of this.

Gwyn Griffiths, Year 5/6 teacher

Before introducing values lessons, please consider the following checklist for introducing a values-based curriculum into your school or classroom. Working through the process will ensure that you adopt a holistic approach to values work, avoiding values lessons being seen as a bolt-on to the curriculum.

Values education will bring tremendous benefits to the climate of your classroom. You have seen that success will come about only if you understand that it is primarily through your behaviour that real improvement will occur. This does not mean that you have to behave unrealistically; just be yourself. If you feel that you aren't living the values, then say so, and say that you are trying. For instance, if the value for the month is patience and a situation arises in which you lose your cool, acknowledge that you did and say that you too are working on the value.

If you are successfully applying values in your school or your classroom, you may want to volunteer to talk about your experience at a staff meeting. You might be asked to do so by other members of staff or the headteacher. The fact that you are being successful will be a recommendation in itself. Remember to relax and be yourself. When giving talks I put a smiley face on a piece of paper to remind me to be me. We are usually at our most influential when we are being ourselves and talking from personal experience. This is what teachers are good at doing and other teachers appreciate it. Long theoretical sessions do not go down well.

A powerful beginning is a few moments of silence. This allows everyone to bring their attention to the session that you are going to lead. It also has the effect of slowing everyone down so that they feel relaxed, a good state to be in for a values discussion.

Before presenting your ideas at a staff meeting, read through the rest of this chapter. Pick out from the checklist what you think are the important elements for other staff members to hear about. Don't have too much material to share at one session and remember to use practical examples to illustrate your points.

You will find it helpful to begin by considering points A and B before moving to section 1.

Checklist for introducing a values-based curriculum

A. Consider the aim of values education

To improve the quality of education by promoting an ethos which is underpinned by core values that support the development of the whole child as a reflective learner.

B. Reflect on terminology

Ethos: refers to the pervasive atmosphere, ambience or climate within your class and within the school. In its broadest sense, the term encompasses all aspects of inclusion, the nature of relationships, the dominant forms of social interaction, the attitudes and expectations of staff, the learning climate, the way that conflicts are resolved, the physical environment, links with parents and the local community, patterns of communication, the nature of pupil involvement, discipline procedures, anti-bullying and anti-racist policies, learning and teaching styles, and the school's underlying philosophy and aims. All of these are rich in their potential to influence the developing values, attitudes and personal qualities of children.

Core values: principles and fundamental convictions that act as general guides to behaviour, enduring beliefs about what is worthwhile, ideals for which one strives, standards by which particular beliefs and actions are judged to be good or desirable.

1. Things to think about

○ Decide why you want to introduce values education. What will the benefits be? What preparation and planning needs to be done? Are there any obstacles? How do you intend to overcome them? I suggest that after reading this book you begin by introducing a few elements. Keep planning simple; you could use a symbol, such as a smiley face, in your daily diary to remind you to model a particular value such as patience. A useful way I have found to model this particular value is to imagine that I am in the middle of the classroom looking at all that is going on. I watch the pupils and myself as we interact. The feeling of being a caring, yet objective observer develops and helps me to respond positively to the children. I see myself having a second or two of reflection before I speak in reply to a question. It is that moment – between thought and action – that helps me to model patience and supports the pupils in learning to respond appropriately. Don't fix your mind on problems; that will put you in a negative frame of mind and inhibit your actions. Be realistic. Don't take on more than you can, and do talk yourself up – remember that you are a champion.

○ Think about whether you are willing to act as a role model and advocate for values education. What demands will this place on you?

○ Consider factors that will impact on how you introduce values education.

'To improve the quality of education by promoting an ethos which is underpinned by core values that support the development of the whole child as a reflective learner.'

These include the age of your pupils, gender mix, special educational needs, social and emotional needs, current behaviour, and when values lessons and activities will take place. How will these affect the introduction of values work?

○ Be clear about the values you wish to emphasise. Ideally, these should be adopted as part of a whole-school process that is led by the headteacher, as the outcome of a staff/governor/parent workshop. In my experience all groups produce very similar lists of values, which are not dependent on race, culture, class or religion. If values education is being introduced in the school by you at this point, explain to others what you are doing and get their support. As others see the effect of your work they will want to become actively involved.

○ A set of universal positive values will emerge. These may include: *honesty, peace, humility, freedom, co-operation, care, love, hope, unity, understanding, respect, simplicity, tolerance, responsibility, courage, friendship, patience, appreciation, trust, faith, happiness, quality* and *thoughtfulness*.

○ Many schools appear to prefer having the focus on one value a month. Decide on the monthly order of these.

○ Remember that the way you introduce values will be dependent on your particular school context – rural or town, large or small, established or new staff, other school priorities – and the needs of your pupils. You must take into account the needs of the adults too.

○ The school cannot promote values if the staff do not value themselves and each other. Considering how your school or class meets the needs of staff is essential. It will model valuing others, showing others respect and being authentic as a person – pupils will soon spot any inconsistency between what you say and what you do.

Here are two lists of suggestions – one for the headteacher and one for the class teacher – for how to support and care for staff.

Headteachers

○ Give regular praise to staff for things that are done well. Remember to write to say thank you sometimes.

○ Praise non-teaching staff, who may feel forgotten.

○ Model the values that you expect staff to model.

○ Ask staff how you can support them, and be seen to take action.

○ Ensure that parts of the school used by staff are comfortable and well maintained – for instance staffroom and toilets.

○ Organise social occasions that staff want.

○ Listen actively to your staff.

○ Be prepared to admit mistakes and to say sorry.

Teachers

○ Allow time to brief fully adults who help you in your class.

○ Remember their birthdays with a card and small gift.

○ Say thank you – often.

○ Say sorry if necessary – show that you are human.

○ Appreciate your helpers in front of the children.

- Model good relationships with the adults – a relaxed, warm, happy relationship between the adults in a class has a marked effect on the pupils' attitudes and behaviour.
- Insist that pupils treat your helpers with courtesy and respect at all times – including when you're not in the class.
- Maintain a sense of fun. Values education should be enjoyable and humour is a prerequisite for effective teaching and learning.

2. Things to work your way through

- Audit your class's institutional values. These are the subtle values that the school imparts, often unintentionally. Are they consistent with the values that you will encourage in the pupils?
- Consider how you greet the pupils. What are your relationships with them like? Do the children feel that you get at them or are they aware that you like them, although you may dislike aspects of their behaviour?
- How do you greet the pupils in the morning and say goodbye to them at the end of the afternoon? Do you treat them all equally?
- Is there an atmosphere of mutual respect in your classroom? Are children always expected to hold doors open for adults to go through or do adults sometimes hold doors open for children?
- Are the pupils expected to use poor-quality toilet facilities? If so, what could be done to make them more attractive? Ask them how they would like their toilets to be. You will be surprised at the improvement in the state of the toilets that follows when the children know you care about this aspect of their school experience. The school council can play an active role in this.
- What messages/posters do pupils see on entering the building or coming through their classroom door? Do they feel welcomed?
- In what style and tone are your class rules written? Are they inclusive and written in a positive tone that emphasises a 'we agree' approach?
- How are teaching assistants treated by you and the pupils? How can relationships be improved?
- How are visitors greeted? Ask them how they feel when in your school or classroom.
- How do you promote a peaceful working atmosphere in your classroom? What noise level do you tolerate? Are you able to resist shouting?
- Is time set aside to listen to the views of the pupils? When?
- How do the pupils understand your expectations of them in terms of behaviour and standards of work?
- What principles underpin your system for rewards and sanctions? Are you consistent in applying them?
- Do you use assessment for learning in a formative way, showing that you value your pupils' work? Do pupils know how to improve their work, and do they feel positive about the way you mark and respond to their work? Here are some ideas about marking and oral feedback that teachers find work:
  - Give evaluative comments that help the child learn how to improve.
  - Whenever possible, give oral feedback when returning work.
  - Give lots of oral feedback in plenary sessions, individually and collectively.
  - Give oral feedback while pupils are engaged in a task.

○ Give opportunities for pupils to reflect.

○ Give opportunities for pupils to read/mark their work.

○ Give wait times so that pupils have the chance to think before answering questions.

○ Use wrong answers to develop understanding.

○ Give opportunities for pupils to formulate questions.

More things to consider

◯ What do displays, the way that your classroom is set out and the general care of your classroom say about your values?

◯ Consider how you can model being reflective and how you will develop this skill in the pupils. Self-reflection is central to the establishment of a class that embodies values. It encourages pupils to develop the skill of being focused on their work and their own attitudes and behaviour. It helps them to understand that when they have a thought that produces feelings they have a choice about the action they take. When they have learned this skill, I have noticed big differences in children who have been quick to be aggressive towards others. They learn that there is a space between thought and action.

◯ I recall a Year 3 boy who was always getting into trouble at lunchtime. He wasn't deliberately badly behaved; he got into scraps because he didn't think. I asked him to try an experiment. I said, 'Look at your fingers and imagine each one is a friend of yours.' We looked at his fingers and imagined who they might be. 'Now,' I said, 'next time you feel yourself losing your temper look at your fingers and, either out loud or in your head, say something to each one – remembering that they are your friends and want to help you. By the time you speak to your last friend – number 10 – you will find that you have got your cool back.' At the time I didn't know if this would work, but everyone said later that his behaviour improved.

◯ Think how both your planned and unplanned work as a headteacher or teacher contributes to the spiritual, moral, social and cultural (SMSC) development of your pupils and to the citizenship curriculum.

◯ Identify subjects and areas of study that make specific contributions to the development of values in your pupils.

◯ Throughout the process of introducing core values, involve as many people as possible – other staff, pupils, families and community.

3. Be a key teacher

◯ Become a key values teacher, someone who will be an advocate for values work. Your enthusiasm and commitment, along with 'walking your talk', will create the impetus that ensures that values work will develop in your class and throughout the school.

◯ Consider offering to act as curriculum leader for values work so that the elements of values education can be carefully co-ordinated.

◯ Give time to analyse the current ethos or climate of your class by determining the elements of good practice that already exist.

◯ Celebrate current good practice. This is the key to encouraging other teachers to develop values-based education. One teacher said to me that in her school

'Self-reflection is central to the establishment of a class that embodies values.'

the staff gave emphasis to respecting pupils, ensuring that they were never criticised. When necessary, inappropriate behaviour was criticised, not the person. Here are some ways of celebrating:

- Use class or school assembly to show that you value all that is of worth – the children, their work, their behaviour, their achievements, their courage, their sporting successes, their qualities.
- Create a special session, perhaps at the end of the day, to celebrate how everyone in the class or school is trying to improve. Chose different aspects such as work, behaviour and relationships.
- Celebrate birthdays with a card that's special to the child – perhaps saying something about a value/quality they have.
- Invite parents/relations/carers in at the end of the day for a celebration tea – children can make cakes or biscuits.
- When good practice areas are identified, they can be built on and extended.

4. Learning and teaching

○ Values cannot be taught in isolation. You should provide experiences and situations in which the class or school can consider and reflect on values, later translating this into action. You need to provide for the implicit and explicit consideration of values. Weave values education across the curriculum so that it isn't seen as something that is part of a particular lesson or assembly. For instance, if you are focusing on co-operation, remember to comment on how the children are co-operating in all lessons. In literacy you could ask them to suggest synonyms for co-operation, and get them to write a creative story or poem about an event where co-operation was shown. In history draw out events and stories that show the advantages of co-operation, such as how the civilian population co-operated to overcome hardship in the Second World War. In geography talk about how people have to co-operate to produce food or cope with natural disasters. In science illustrate how scientists have co-operated with each other in space research.

○ Besides ensuring that values are integral across the curriculum, think how you will create situations in which values can be thought about in greater depth. This can be done by introducing values in a programme of school assemblies, or, if this is not practical, by introducing them during a designated lesson. Some teachers do this during Circle Time. Although values cannot be taught but are caught, I recommend that you plan a programme of lessons to create opportunities for personal reflection and moral discourse, including an appropriate activity to promote understanding. Teaching and learning about values takes places in the following steps:

- By teachers explaining the meaning of a value. Stories are an excellent way of helping pupils to understand the meaning of a value. For the value of co-operation try, for instance, using the story 'The Chopsticks and the Chinese Warrior' from *Showing another Way*, a collection of assemblies for junior children by David Downton and Mike Sandy (see page 59).
- Pupils being guided by the teacher to reflect on the value and relate it to their own behaviour and experience. Pupils enjoy thinking about their behaviour, why they do things and how they can do things differently. This kind of practical philosophy gives the teacher an opportunity to talk about

"Today's value is honesty."

how they themselves think and behave, reinforcing the positive relationship between teacher and child.

  ○ By pupils being encouraged to use the value to guide their own actions in and out of the classroom.

'Values education develops emotional literacy, the ability of a pupil to think and talk about their emotional responses.'

Points to remember

A. You will gain a deepening of your own understanding of values as you introduce them.

B. Highlight one value each month. Make a prominent visual display of the value as a poster in your class.

C. Consider holding class assemblies. These are excellent ways for pupils to relate the value to their own experience and make an appropriate presentation to their class or other classes.

D. Values are imbibed when children can relate them to real-life situations, so use incidents that happen during the school day. Talk with the children about how they can play more happily with each other. Build on their ideas and don't wait until there is an unhappy incident before talking about appropriate behaviour.

E. Allow time during assemblies and values lessons for silent reflection. This encourages pupils to go within themselves to learn to become calm and focused and to control their thoughts and reactions.

F. Reflection can be used as an aid to learning in any lesson. Begin by reflecting about what you and the pupils hope to achieve during the session. This puts everyone in a positive, can do frame of mind. Boys seem to benefit greatly from guidance about the process of reflection. Generally speaking, this is something girls do more readily.

G. Use story-telling. This is an excellent medium for helping pupils to understand the meaning of a value.

H. Use a variety of teaching and learning styles to ensure that all pupils are engaged in the thinking process. Values lessons are a form of philosophy for children. Pupils consider real-life situations, reflect on their own behaviour and responses and listen to those of others.

I. Values education develops emotional literacy, the ability of a pupil to think and talk about their emotional responses. This process enables children to gain self-discipline and take responsibility for their actions.

J. A by-product of values education is that the self-esteem and confidence of the pupils improves, along with their oral skills.

K. The Socratic method of questioning, nowadays known as 'rich questioning', extends children's thinking, deepens understanding and shows the children that you value their comments. During a lesson on respect, ask questions but tell the children not to put their hands up as you are going to select people to answer. Give them ample time to think before they give answers and don't give the impression that you have a right answer in your head which you expect the children to guess. Build an atmosphere in which all answers are valued as helping the class to make progress – explain that we learn from our mistakes. Ask open-ended questions that help to extend thinking, such as 'Could you explain . . . ?' 'How would you feel if . . . ?' 'Why does . . . ?'

L. Encourage non-teaching staff to use the value of the month in their work with pupils.

M. Encourage all staff who work in your school or classroom to model the values through their own behaviour. This may not be easy. It is important to be authentic and to admit lapses.

N. Ensure that values are woven through the fabric of the curriculum. For instance, in PE is everyone demonstrating the value of respect for self, each other and equipment?

O. Newsletters to parents are very beneficial; they ensure that parents understand and can support what you are doing at school. Explain what the value of the month is and how they can develop the value at home. Parents respond very positively to this kind of involvement.

P. Workshops for parents are also a useful way of engaging the community. If governors take part in these sessions, that demonstrates the importance that is being placed on the work. Organise a workshop around a value for the month and invite parents to come, saying that it will help them to help their children to get the most out of their time at school. Be careful not to put parents off by appearing to be patronising. You should not approach the workshop by intending to teach the parents – they might teach you a thing or two. If the theme of the evening is respect, it is vital that you demonstrate this quality throughout the workshop. Start with refreshments, but avoid wine. (I once had a very strange but hilarious evening when I was invited to give a talk to parents who had all been given generous quantities of wine before I started.) Make your letter of invitation a warm one. (See page 60 for a photocopiable letter class teachers can use.)

Here are some ideas that you could adapt for a parents' workshop:

- Create a peaceful, reflective atmosphere by playing an appropriate piece of music on tape or CD. I often use a CD by Bliss called Through these Eyes (www.blissfulmusic.com).

- Introduce the session, saying that its purpose is to inform the parents about values education and to have an enjoyable time together.

- Ask the parents to think about what qualities they would like their children to have when they leave school.

- Ask them in 2s or 3s to discuss and choose what they think are the two most important of those qualities.

- List these qualities on a flipchart. Explain what a value is. Talk about the qualities on the list as values. (These values could become the basis for your school's statement of values.)

- Next, discuss ways in which the school and parents can help their children to develop positive values.

- Talk about how the school is promoting a positive school ethos. Also talk about what the school will be doing in assemblies and lesson times.

- Give the parents an opportunity to experience quiet reflection so that they will understand what their children will be doing.

- Finally, allow time for questions and for emphasising that values education is a partnership between home and school.

Q. At induction sessions for new parents of pupils, explain your policy on values education.

5. Skills, knowledge, attitudes and understanding

- Decide on the range of skills, knowledge, attitudes and understanding that you wish to develop in the pupils.

- Remember that you are encouraging the holistic development of the pupil. This includes the spiritual world of the pupil – the inner world of thoughts and feelings. Through encouragement of their spiritual development the pupil learns how to observe their thoughts and to think positively.

- Focusing attention and actively listening whilst sitting still are skills that promote reflective learning and good interpersonal skills. To promote positive listening, start by showing the children how to sit. Encourage them to sit with straight backs. (It is not good for children to sit for long periods with poor posture.) Children soon develop the habit of sitting correctly. This aids effective breathing, which keeps the brain supplied with adequate oxygen. (The brain uses 70% of the oxygen we breathe.) We can concentrate for longer periods if we are breathing properly, using the whole of our lungs rather than just the top sections. Good classroom ventilation is important too.

Next, ask the children to think about what you are saying, not just to look at you. Children easily acquire the habit of looking at their teacher to give the impression that they are listening. Asking children questions directly, without expecting hands to go up, is a way of helping them to listen actively. Remember not to talk for long at a time. Children are often expected to focus on teacher talk for too long. A rough guide to the average concentration span is to take a child's age and double it (e.g. for a 4-year-old, 8 minutes). A useful tactic, which I use in my teaching, is to stop after a few minutes, and ask the children to be reflective, to think about what has been said in the lesson. Do they understand? What have the main points been? Then ask some relevant questions and invite comments before you continue the lesson. Punctuating the lesson in this way is a tremendous aid to learning because it prevents the child from being passive. Long-term learning is promoted through frequent opportunities to reflect and to recall.

- Lasting learning is associated with positive emotions and feelings. In our society people suffer from overload and fragmentation – forms of chaos. A values approach creates stability and empowers the individual to be in control of their reactions to situations, avoiding a negative response.

- The development of a class council, which supports the school's council, has the potential for giving pupils opportunities to feel involved in decision-making that affects the life of the school. There are lots of issues that a class council can be involved in. These include reviewing the class rules and reporting findings to the teacher; effective classroom management – giving out the jobs that make a happy and well-organised classroom; meeting the headteacher to give a report on life in the classroom (e.g. what children are working on, what they are finding easy or more challenging); deciding how to make the classroom happier, quieter, more peaceful or more fun.

6. Benefits for the pupils

○ Identify the benefits that pupils will experience as values education is introduced. These should include improved concentration, better pupil behaviour, and improved social and academic standards.

○ Consider issues of achievement, quality of learning, the raising of self-esteem and the development of reflective practices.

7. Final thoughts and reminders

○ Ensure that the process of introducing and developing values education is well planned, monitored, evaluated and celebrated in order to keep the process alive and constantly under review.

○ Throughout the process of developing values education, share the development with parents and the wider school community.

'Maintaining an ethos in the classroom that is positive and all-inclusive, incorporating equality, will help children gain the most from values lessons.'

Maintaining an ethos in the classroom that is positive and all-inclusive, incorporating equality, will help children gain the most from values lessons. It is important that any approach to class management is in line with the values being taught. Children will soon feel secure and able to share their thoughts, feelings and experiences when they know that these are always welcomed and valued.

Working through and considering the advice in the checklist above will prepare you for creating a classroom climate that embraces values education. Here are some of the benefits that have been identified by teachers using values education.

Benefits for the pupils of values education

○ Behaving more calmly and purposefully.

○ Gaining ability to concentrate and reflect on their own behaviour.

○ Becoming more self-aware and self-accepting.

○ Being more considerate to others and less ego centred.

○ Taking greater responsibility for their own behaviour and realising that they have choices.

○ Improving their listening skills.

○ Enabling them to gain more from their lessons because they are thinking more before taking action.

○ Improving their self-confidence and self-esteem.

○ Helping them to know themselves better and become able to relate to others more effectively.

To conclude this chapter, I have selected a case study for you to consider. It explains how a first school in Oxford has worked through the process of introducing values, adapting it to its own circumstances.

This is the engaging and revealing story of how the staff of Windmill First School introduced and are developing values education. The school's newly appointed deputy head, Karen Errington, was catapulted into the role of acting head. She introduced the school to values education. The process was continued and developed when the new headteacher, Lindsey Weimers, joined the school and Karen returned to being a class-based deputy. This is their story.

Case study: Windmill First School

Below are outlined the seven stages we went through in introducing a values-based approach to learning:
- Identifying a need for change.
- Visualising our ideal school.
- Celebrating our current strengths.
- Identifying areas for development.
- Practical organisation to implement changes.
- Producing a values policy and guidelines.
- Supporting staff.

Stage 1 – Identifying a need for change
Within our school community there was a growing unease with the curriculum we were offering to our pupils and to the pressures of life in the twenty-first century for both adults and children.
- Because of league tables judging school performance in the three Rs, there was an initial concern that these subjects were starting to be valued above others.
- All teachers sensed an acute shortage of time that was affecting the way we related to each other in class, school and the broader community. We were proud of our school community and did not want to lose our good relationships.
- Children were becoming less likely to experience quiet and still times. We noticed, as teachers and parents, that children found it hard to sit still and focus unless watching a video.
- We were conscious that many media messages show us quick fixes for short-lived material happiness.
- We wanted to find a fresh way to address behaviour issues – one that inspired pupils to choose their own moral codes and would enable them to contribute positively to the world.

Stage 2 – Visualising our ideal school
From both formal and informal conversation with teachers, parents, governors and children, it became apparent that the school needed to 'regain control' and start constructing a school day that addressed the issues of concern. We decided to start by using our next inset day to visualise our ideal school and create a set of new aims for our school. We invited governors, parents, the caretaker, cleaners, lunchtime supervisors, teaching assistants, office managers and teachers to join in.

- To start the session, we asked ourselves this question: If you could give a child one gift/quality, what would it be? Responses included self-respect, peace of mind, tolerance, high self-esteem, happiness. Not one person said 'L6 in the National Curriculum SATs'.
- We decided that our aims and future school experience had to reflect these desires. We felt excited – many teachers were remembering the fundamental reasons why they entered teaching: to make a difference to someone's life; to educate character; to enhance body, mind and spirit.
- Research and common sense reassured us that when children feel good about themselves, they learn more. Furthermore, adults who have good interpersonal and intrapersonal skills achieve more. We predicted that by the development of a values-based approach to learning, our pupils might achieve better academic results too.

Stage 3 – Celebrating our current strengths
It was important that at this point we reminded ourselves that we are good at what we do and that our future development was a matter of refining skilled practice.

Case study

Case study

Case study: Windmill First School continued

Stage 4 – Identifying areas for development

○ An audit revealed that most PSHE time was a matter of fire-fighting – an incident occurred, usually at lunchtime, and then a discussion would result. At this point pupils' emotions were often out of control and it was impossible to have an open and reasoned discussion with them.
  ⇨ We wanted quality time allocated to debate important issues calmly and honestly, to give pupils the opportunity to learn and reflect on their own behaviour.

○ Whole-school assemblies were isolated events, which met a legal requirement and gave teachers free time.
  ⇨ We wanted assemblies to inspire us – all of us! We wanted them to be a celebration. But most of all we needed assemblies that were a meaningful and worthwhile experience, enriching school life and guiding us all.

○ Increasingly life at home and school involved rushing around with little time to relax and reflect.
  ⇨ We wanted to create periods of quiet and stillness in which pupils could explore their inner worlds, develop concentration and focus more easily.

○ We ourselves should be role models. As a staff we realised that we needed to try to act consistently in line with the values we wished to teach. The way we are as individuals will teach our pupils more than any discussion we could have with them. If we expect our pupils to treat each other with respect, we must demonstrate respect to them and to each other as staff and parents.
  ⇨ This was the most challenging area of development as it entailed raising our consciousness.

Stage 5 – Practical organisation to implement changes

Deciding which values to adopt for our school

We chose a two-year cycle of twenty-two values – many of these values were identified at the initial inset day, when we had listed replies to the question 'Which quality would you give a child?' However, we also chose some qualities because we had teaching resources to support them. This list is reviewed, and if necessary adapted, each September.

Stage 6 – Producing a values policy and guidelines

Guidelines were created and produced during a series of staff meetings involving governors. At these meetings the following were identified:

○ the needs of the pupils and the school community;
○ the potential role of the school assembly;
○ activities to support values-based education;
○ how to teach a successful values lesson;
○ a strategy to create a school council.

Later in the year we revisited our school aims and produced measurable criteria for each one so that we could assess if we were making progress towards our vision.

The values lesson

Each month a class lesson takes place during which the teacher and pupils explore what a particular value means to them. In Key Stage 2 this will last approximately ninety minutes to two hours, and in Key Stage 1 between forty-five minutes and ninety minutes. Often the stimulus will be a story; sometimes it will be a personal account by the teacher. The lesson aims to present the value to the pupils and make clear how it can affect them and others.

All lessons, whether Key Stage 1 or Key Stage 2, follow a similar outline – this is encouraged through the use of a whole-school planning sheet (see page 61).

The first section of this sheet informs the teachers about the key aspects to cover with their class.

Case study

Case study: Windmill First School continued

The second section, 'Reflection', refers to silent sitting, in which the teacher and children prepare themselves for the lesson and promote a sense of wellbeing. This usually lasts between two and five minutes.

The third section, 'Stimulus', is an initial story, personal recounting, reflection, photograph or news report that will capture the interest of the class and inspire further discussion. This part of the lesson varies in length. If the stimulus is a story, it may take up to twenty minutes.

In the fourth section, 'Discussion', the teacher carefully considers key questions that will focus the pupils' thinking on the main concept of the lesson. Discussions last from fifteen to sixty minutes, depending on the pupils and their interest level. This is the part of the lesson where pupil opinion should be listened to – not teacher opinion. The teacher needs to be flexible and willing to deviate from the plan should the pupils begin to take the discussion in another valid direction. What is important is quality of discussion and understanding, not quantity.

In the final section pupils carry out a piece of work on the value. This may take anything from thirty to sixty minutes, depending on the activity. Be prepared for the pupils to be enthusiastic and have their own ideas of what follow-up work should take place.

To conclude a values lesson, pupils are brought back together to share and celebrate work. A final reflection may take place, picking up on one of the key discussion points.

The use of reflection
Time is allotted for periods of short reflection (2–5 minutes) during whole-school assemblies, class assemblies and values lessons and on other occasions during the school day. We find reflection is a powerful tool to increase concentration and readiness to learn; it also creates a calm space for pupils and teacher within a busy school day.

Stage 7 – Supporting staff
Whole-school assemblies
Assemblies are now central to the life of the school. They are based on the month's value. Many of the world's faiths have excellent stories that relate directly to values. Staff attending assemblies are presented with examples of how to discuss values, they hear stories they could develop in class and see partnership and mutual respect between teacher and pupils modelled.

Increasing teacher understanding and confidence
Each month teachers complete a values planning sheet that breaks down the month's value into key points. This increases our confidence. It would be difficult to teach a value such as simplicity or humility without a specific starting point.

The headteacher and values co-ordinator spend time talking to staff and reassuring them that in order to teach values we do not need to be perfect. In fact, revealing to the pupils that we are not perfect may inspire them to try harder.

The first thing we all recognise when starting values education is that there is no 'quick fix' approach. What we are addressing is something fundamental that ultimately taps into each individual's understanding of who they are. It can be very challenging. Each strategy we use needs to be seen in a long-term context. Each is on-going and needs continual reinforcement and revisiting. We would be the first to admit that we still have a long way to go. However, we are delighted with the success of values education so far.

Reality?

With excellent examples fresh in your mind, I sense that you may by now be saying something like this:

> OK, it all sounds ideal but life isn't like that. They ought to be at our school at lunchtime or wander into the boys' toilets after a football match when they have lost! How would they introduce values education in a very challenging school?

This is a fair question. To reassure you, during the last three years I have been working with a dedicated group of teachers who make up Oxfordshire's school improvement team (OSIT). I too have worked in challenging schools and have experienced extremes of pupil behaviour. I have learned that working from a values base means that we must be consistent; have high expectations; and be definite and positive, not reacting negatively when pupils are challenging. Here is some advice about dealing with the hard class given by Louise McGinty, one of the teachers in the team:

> Be positive. We are wonderful! You must make the children sure that you believe it even on bad days. Smile therapy works here. Put a smile on your face and say something and it will appear more positive to the recipient. Children reflect what they experience, and whilst we cannot change some of the external factors contributing to their behaviour, we can make it a more positive experience for them. 'We are wonderful' wall charts help for the times it really goes well; make them a real collective pat on the back and make the rewards for filling in something on the chart extra special. Be selective over when rewards are given out; praise will be less effective if over-used. Remember, it is not really brilliant to sit on a chair correctly; it is what we expect. We want the children's behaviour to exceed our expectations for them to gain maximum rewards.

> Teach the children silent cheers, where they just mime the cheer for someone or something. A pat on the back can be a silent one, as can a round of applause. At the end of the day celebrate good behaviour. Reflect on the positive steps taken and on how we can all make the classroom a better place to be in.

The starting point, as demonstrated by Louise, is maintaining a positive attitude with the children. There is no quick fix and there will be times when you feel like despairing. At such times it is important to have a colleague with whom you can share your frustrations, who will listen and be supportive.

Here is one way of tackling a challenging situation at school. It uses a creative process called *appreciative inquiry*.

Appreciative inquiry

○ Step 1 Audit the 'problem'. Make sure you understand what the real problem is and are not diverted by its symptom. Get as many people involved in the audit as possible, including the pupils. Work in pairs to explore the issue. Have a listening dialogue; don't impose ideas on one another. Note down the positive ideas that arise from discussions.

○ Step 2 Visualise. Visualise a situation in which the problem does not occur. What is happening? What are children and adults doing? Share each other's positive thoughts.

○ Step 3 Design the solution. From the positive thoughts the solution will become known. Now weave the solution into the practice of the school.

○ Step 4 Commitment. Commit to paper what has been agreed and get everyone to commit themselves to making the vision work in practice.

○ Step 5 Communicate. Communicate your ideas to the school's community and set a date when the issue will be reviewed to ensure that the original problem identified has been resolved.

Appreciative inquiry is a value-based process, working from the positive. It involves appreciating each person as an equal member of the group. Sometimes the best ideas are in the minds of the newest member of staff or the one who is shy. The processes for so-called problem-solving usually favour the more dominant personalities or those who hold the greatest status in a group. The solutions arrived at in those circumstances do not necessarily command the respect of the majority and there may be more problems at the implementation stage.

Much of the work in this chapter depends on one crucial factor — your taking care of yourself. The next chapter explains how you can do that, and how to feel more positive as a teacher.

'Sometimes the best ideas are in the minds of the newest member of staff or the one who is shy.'

Chapter 4
How to maintain a positive reflective manner

'At its best teaching is the medium that helps to create a civilised society.'

Values education is what attracted me to come and teach at this school. It happens all across the school because of our headteacher: she is positive with us all the time and, in turn, we are positive with the children. I think it's really important because it helps children to develop their own sense of morality.

Emma Leadbetter, Year 2/3 teacher

Are you caring for yourself?

At courses on values education I often begin by asking teachers if they are caring for themselves. Usually, at the beginning of the course everyone seems relaxed and happy, but a few moments of asking questions reveal levels of anxiety and disaffection. You may care to think about the following questions:

- ◗ How has your day been so far?
- ◗ What have you done since getting up?
- ◗ How have you been feeling this week?
- ◗ How much time have you given to yourself?

I have often been very surprised by the comments and feelings that have been shared – not all of them positive. Most teachers, it seems, often feel overwhelmed by the amount of work that they have to do, especially planning. Many primary teachers say that they teach for nearly 100 per cent of the school day and feel guilty that they don't complete all the tasks that they intended to do, so they go home feeling frustrated and inadequate.

The problem seems to be that during the last decade teachers have been subjected to unprecedented change. They are under tremendous pressure because of educational reforms and the ever-increasing demands of accountability. Also, teachers often have to deal with pupil and family problems. I have become increasingly concerned at the number of teachers who need to take time away from school because of stress. What can you do to avoid excessive stress and maintain a stable inner world? How can you care for others if you don't care for yourself?

I believe that teaching is the most important job in the world. Teachers are responsible for shaping the future. Good teaching is a conversation from generation to generation about matters of significance. At its best teaching is the medium that helps to create a civilised society – surely the major aim of education in the twenty-first century.

In order to take on this pivotal role in society you must feel content. Impossible, I hear you say! Yes, it is difficult. Increasing numbers of teachers want to find ways to be effective in the classroom without experiencing the feeling of inadequacy brought about by work overload. Teachers are concerned about the self-esteem of their pupils but often forget to nurture their own. Do you? I think, with practice, all of us can be more content and peaceful. The more peaceful we can be, the more peaceful our pupils will be. Let us be clear about what peace is.

> Peace is your original quality. In its purest form, peace is inner silence. It consists of positive thoughts, pure feelings and good wishes. To have peace you need patience. When you are peaceful, you create an atmosphere of peace. Peace in the world can only be realised when there is peace in our minds.

How can we begin to have this quality of peacefulness? The following is a checklist of suggestions that I have found work in practice:

① Each teaching day, set aside quiet times for personal reflection. These times do not have to be long – one or two minutes are often enough. When and where, I hear you ask. Well, even a visit to the toilet can provide the opportunity. During a day in the classroom the brain is bombarded with thousands of thoughts as we cope with the demands of the curriculum and streams of questions from our pupils. This overload of mental activity leads to tension and stress. To reduce this we need to slow down the brain's unnecessary mental traffic, which often includes negative thoughts, by practising what may be termed traffic control. This means remaining still, standing or sitting, and going inside yourself to be the observer of your thoughts. As you do this, please don't judge your thoughts, or suppress or try to control them; simply watch them. As you do so, you will notice that your thoughts will begin to slow down and you will feel much more calm and relaxed. In this process let go of waste or negative thoughts that crowd your mind. All too often we allow our minds to focus on the one negative thing that happened in the class, rather than remembering the many positive things. How many times have you gone home remembering the child or parent who was negative rather than all the interactions that were pleasant and positive? You may find this process difficult at first, but regular practice makes it become a habit. Practice will make you skilled, with the result that you will develop a more peaceful, contented internal world and become less affected by the demands of the external world.

② Get up earlier! (Please don't shut the book at this point.) Most of us get up after our alarm rings and immediately go into action. We don't pause for a second because we have a list of things to achieve before we go to school: children's lunches to prepare, breakfast to get ready, household jobs to be completed. All this means we leave for school in a state that is often not remotely peaceful – especially if we have an arduous drive ahead. The solution to this is to set the alarm half an hour earlier and get up. Make a drink of tea or coffee, or perhaps just get some water, and then find somewhere to sit quietly and go through the process of traffic control described above. Remember that this time is not wasted time; it is a special time for you. Where you sit is important – not in the bedroom because this place is associated with sleep. In the summer I often sit outside. I have a friend in the Middle East who has told me that this has been the key for her getting through some very difficult days working in potentially dangerous situations. Hopefully, you won't have to face such an extreme. I promise that after a while you will feel that something special is missing from your day if you don't start it in this quiet, reflective way. Remember, you don't have to sit in any particular way or think about anything in particular – just be the observer of your thoughts and gently put positive thoughts in your mind when negative ones arise.

③ Stop beating yourself up! Many teachers seem to be self-critical and dissatisfied – as if they have a negative voice constantly chattering in their head. To address this, start to make a daily list of things that have gone well instead of going home remembering the one or two things that went badly. We think about these negative experiences again and again so that they become like films running continuously on the screen of our mind. Whenever we feel stressed the film starts and so do the negative feelings and emotions that go with it. To stop these hurtful thoughts, acknowledge them as they arise – do not suppress them – but gently tell yourself that you don't want to give them any attention. Think happy, positive thoughts and with practice the old films will fade. Remember that you can only do your best and you can't be responsible for the thoughts and feelings of others.

④ Time for creative imagining, we are told, is good for us. Day-dreaming is necessary for our wellbeing, yet as teachers we often stop pupils from doing it. At the end of the day, just before going to sleep, enjoy a few moments consciously creating some really happy, positive thoughts and images. This habit will help you to sleep peacefully and wake more full of energy. It stops you from spending those minutes before sleeping worrying about the events of the day. You are also less likely to wake up during the night thinking about jobs that need to be completed. What sort of happy thoughts, you may wonder. These will vary depending on what scenes help you to feel, relaxed, happy and calm. My thoughts usually take me to a scene of natural beauty. Each year I try to spend time in the mountains and it is images of these that I often bring to mind. Don't struggle to create images on the screen of your mind that don't come naturally – you may be in a poor mood. At those times, don't think about the thoughts you are having – just watch them. Distance yourself from them, and as you distance yourself you will disconnect the emotions that you are feeling from the thoughts. I know that this sounds complicated, but it does work. You will then feel more at ease and be able to create more positive thoughts and images.

⑤ Help each other. As a staff, care for each other by having a school policy for mutual care. We all cope better when we have a strong feeling of community support. To achieve this some schools do the following:
   ○ Give thought to making the staffroom a comfortable place where staff feel relaxed. Attention has to be given to ensuring that it is not a tatty room

'As a staff, care for each other by having a school policy for mutual care. We all cope better when we have a strong feeling of community support.'

cluttered with school notices. Instead, transform it into an aesthetically pleasing area with comfortable chairs, pictures, pleasant cups or mugs, a water dispenser and plants.

○ Provide times for staff to have massage or other appropriate therapies after school. This makes the statement that the school cares for the staff and wants them to have opportunities to remain both mentally and physically healthy. Of course, you don't have to organise staff massage; simply talk about how you care for each other and take actions that show you do.

Schools may need to set up a hierarchy of roles so that everyone is clear about what everyone does, but they should never have hierarchies of relationships. All staff should feel equal to each other. Good relationships are at the heart of effective schools and these come about because of a warm feeling of community engendered by equality. On a day-to-day basis staff can look after each other in the following ways:

○ Giving up time to listen to colleagues – this shows that you care.

○ Taking an interest in others and what they do outside school.

○ Offering to help when that is not expected.

○ Remembering to speak positively about colleagues, avoiding a complaining culture.

○ Making all staff feel included and valued.

⑥ Live in 'up time' rather than in 'down time'. What are you thinking about now? Are you thinking about the ideas written on this page, or are your thoughts instead in the past or the future? We spend a large proportion of our time thinking about the past or the future – this is called 'down time'. By living in down time we miss the pleasures and opportunities of the present. 'Up time' is the present time, this moment – it is the only real time. If you would like to experience up time, follow this exercise.

Experience the pleasures of up time

Time yourself for three minutes. If possible, go out into a garden. If not, walk around the house. Concentrate on paying attention to the present. Look at the sights round you, and be aware of the sounds and the smells. Make this your special time – a time to experience the now. At the end of the three minutes, reflect on the experience. With practice you will find that you will spend more of your time in up time and will worry less about the past and future.

⑦ Do what's important, not what's urgent. Do you give your time to the important things of life or do you attend to the urgent? I must admit that I have often found myself attending to e-mails when I should have been attending to an important piece of writing. Writing a 'to do' list and then deciding what is most important is the first step. The next is attending to the important things first and not filling your time with the urgent. This habit reduces stress and brings greater satisfaction.

'Values education enables us to help children to develop spiritually.'

⑧ Next, I want to make a suggestion that I know some teachers will find challenging. Some of the words and ideas may not be familiar to you. I have said that I believe values education enables us to help children to develop spiritually. Spiritual education develops human potential – including personality, emotions and fundamental characteristics and capacities such as love, peace, wonder, joy, creativity, aspiration, idealism, the search for meaning, values and commitment and the capacity to respond to the challenges of change, hardship, danger, suffering and despair. Some people develop spiritually by being a part of a world faith; others look for other means. My last suggestion is to develop a *spiritual tool kit*. Three friends helped me to develop this. When you have read about it I hope you will spend a few minutes thinking about how it could help you and your work with your class or school.

I find one of the easiest ways to understand spirituality is to think of it as your personal inner world of thoughts and feelings – a world that is real for it is your consciousness, but cannot be seen. Only the results of your thoughts and feelings can be seen, in the form of actions which create the material world of objects, such as cars, clothes, entertainment and so on. In caring for yourself and others, your tool kit will be very useful.

The tool kit was devised following a series of meetings between three teachers – Linda and John Heppenstall and myself – and the sculptress Wendy Marshall. We explored the notion of spirituality in the context of our school's values education policy. I hope that you will find the spiritual tool kit helpful and will come to see values education as a process to enable children to develop spirituality. It is a series of steps that will enable you to develop your knowledge, skills and understanding of spirituality.

The purpose of fostering spirituality is to help pupils become aware of their spiritual nature, which incorporates the qualities through which they can lead more fulfilled, and happier lives.

The spiritual tool kit

Step 1
Have a clear understanding of what spirituality means
Begin to develop an understanding of your inner world of thoughts, feelings and emotions. This is your spiritual world. A clear understanding of your own spirituality will enable you to develop an understanding of the concept which is at the heart of values education and of caring for yourself.

What is spirituality?
We are beings made up of body and spirit. We are aware of our bodies and a moment's thought will make us aware that we are conscious beings, with ideas, feelings and emotions. This is the essence of our spirituality. We can think of ways to develop the physical body or the intellectual mind, but what about the spirit? If the spirit is not developed we grow into incomplete adults, just as if the body and mind are not developed we will not be able to lead full and contented lives.

How can we begin to understand what our spirit is? Imagine a delicious chocolate wrapped in silver paper with an almond centre. The wrapping is like the body, attractive and eyecatching. The chocolate represents the conscious mind. The almond at the centre of our being represents our thoughts and feelings – our spirit. This spirit is the source of our values, qualities and virtues. These include love, trust, truth and peace. The spirit needs to be nurtured to have its full effect on the quality of our own and other people's lives.

Step 2
Get to know your spiritual self
Quiet reflection is the route to this destination. Make a set time, an appointment, to be with yourself. Begin to explore your spiritual self by sitting quietly in a positive way, focusing on aspects of yourself which create good feelings. Make sure you create thoughts and images that do not lead to a critical frame of mind.

If negative thoughts occur, acknowledge them and move on to concentrate on positive ones. For people of faith, their prayer life may fulfil this role.

Meetings with yourself
Giving yourself regular, quiet, reflective times puts you in touch with your spiritual self, creates wellbeing, and helps you to be in control of your life.

During reflection, consider qualities such as humility, respect, responsibility and love. What do they mean to you? Are you aware of them within yourself? They are present, but they may be hidden. Over time you will come to know and appreciate your spiritual identity. The method is simple.

Step 3
Have a desire to grow spiritually
Getting to know yourself is hard work, a lifetime's journey. Set out on that journey. The rewards are enormous; you will become more self-aware and self-confident. Your teaching will improve and will be less stressful as you will concentrate on the positive rather than on perceived failures. Learn to praise yourself.

When you are on this journey, you consciously and unconsciously begin to show your inner self, your best self, to your pupils. You will become a model for them, and children will recognise and respond to this. For instance, as you develop the quality of respect within yourself, you may see the children differently, as equal beings sharing a learning experience with you. They will notice and respond with respect.

The more you raise your inner, spiritual qualities, the more you will raise the self-respect and self-esteem of your pupils. When you appreciate your pupils, you are honest with them and you trust them. Without self-esteem there is no progress in learning.

Step 4
Communicate with others on a spiritual level
As you become more aware of your spiritual self, you will find you are more likely to communicate with others spiritually. You will begin to see people at a level that is not dominated by appearance. You will be less likely to think of people from the viewpoint of your own selfish ego.

How do we communicate with people?
Usually we communicate at three points:
- appearance;
- personality (emotion);
- spirituality.

Communication via appearance is pleasant but transient.

Communication via personality and emotion can be very pleasant but also painful.

Communication via spirituality is much more satisfying. It constitutes a deeper connection, involving unconditional love and acceptance. When you communicate with people at this level, the deeper connection will be evident in everything you do and say. It will manifest itself in your interactions and your relationships.

Communicating with pupils spiritually
When you communicate like this, you will find that children respond appropriately without realising why. They will have respect for you, they will consider you to be a good teacher, and you will find the job of teaching becomes easier and more fulfilling.

Step 5
Actively teach others
Plan to develop the pupils' ability to work on all the steps given up to now by developing the strategies outlined with them during time spent working on values.

Benefits of using the spiritual tool kit

The benefits of using the spiritual tool kit are many and include improved interpersonal and intrapersonal relationships. The latter is the relationship we have with ourselves. Also, quality of work is improved as a result of reflection and self-discipline. Pupils remain on task during lessons because of the work-related atmosphere that is created; they are relaxed but alert and focused. Listening skills improve, as do presentation skills.

Staff report impressive benefits to them as they are less stressed. They are able to focus on good teaching.

For us to be positive role models for pupils we have to feel good and positive about ourselves. Our self-esteem should be high and our internal world secure. Caring for ourselves can take many forms and includes being aware of our physical, mental and spiritual selves. It is not selfish to give ourselves both time and space; paradoxically, when we do that we will be able to give more to others and become more able to cope.

Before going on to read the next chapter about nurturing values through assemblies, give yourself a peaceful opportunity to think about the ideas in the spiritual tool kit.

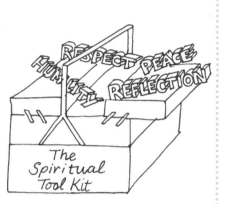

The Spiritual Tool Kit

Chapter 5
How you can create a values-based assembly

I was amazed to find that assemblies provide an accessible but meaningful context for discussion with my early years children. I didn't think they would be able to access the words, but by using the value word together with others with the same meaning in contexts that are familiar to young children, they took on board the meaning, application and vocabulary. It is wonderful to overhear children saying things to one another like 'I think it's so nice when we have a bit of peace time' or 'It's so noisy in here I think we need a bit of peace time.' Not only does values education help children in their everyday lives, but also it gives them a window on to the wider world.

Jennie Woolridge, Reception/Year 1 teacher

'A high-quality values-based school assembly is one of the most important and enjoyable aspects of values education.'

As you can see from Jennie's comments, central to the development of values education is the provision of good-quality assemblies. Do you look on assemblies as a chore or do you look forward to them as an opportunity to nurture the ethos of the school? In this chapter you will find practical help for creating an excellent values-based assembly. You will discover how to transform your school assemblies so that you, other staff and pupils will look forward to them.

What is an assembly?
An assembly is when the school community, or a part of it, meets together to share aspects of life that are of worth. An assembly, a legal requirement since 1944, usually contains an act of worship.

I believe a high-quality values-based school assembly is one of the most important and enjoyable aspects of values education. It has tremendous potential to nurture a positive school ethos that emphasises care for the self and for others and the pursuit of all forms of excellence. It aims to create, develop and sustain a sense of community that affirms the school's identity and aspirations. This helps the school to develop a sense of harmony.

Benefits for pupils of a value-based assembly
Benefits include the following:

- A clearer understanding of themselves – why they think and behave as they do.
- Improved awareness of the needs of others.
- Helps pupils to understand the feelings of others.
- Raises pupils' self-esteem and confidence.
- Develops pupils' spiritual intelligence – their inner world of thoughts and feelings.

○ Helps pupils to feel calm, happy and purposeful.

○ The positive atmosphere creates the climate for raising achievement and standards.

○ The assembly contributes to their developing personal autonomy and contentment.

○ The assembly improves their behaviour as they feel valued and respected.

There are benefits for the teachers too. The leader of the assembly and all adults taking part should feel that the assembly is a special time. Ideally, it is a time that is considered valuable because of the opportunity it gives to be still, to reflect, and to be at peace. It is a time set apart from the normal routine, in which staff feel valued as people.

What makes a good assembly?

Location

First, consider the physical setting for an assembly. A pleasant environment helps to create a good atmosphere. Care over detail is important. Make sure that the heating, ventilation, comfort and decoration of the room are appropriate. Then think about the way in which you and other staff will behave in the assembly in order to create that special atmosphere.

Things to think about

○ Could the leader of the assembly be seated in a reflective attitude as the pupils arrive for the assembly?

○ Pupils' involvement in the assembly.

○ A display so that everyone knows the value for the month.

○ Music to help create a calm and reflective mood.

○ How the pupils and staff will be seated – rows, circle, horseshoe?

○ A music centre and speakers – if funds allow.

○ Black-out and spot lighting – if available.

○ Microphones so that speakers can be heard.

○ All adults should model the behaviour that they expect of pupils.

Underlying the points above is a wish to create an environment for an assembly in which everyone is 'walking the talk' of values education.

The leader

Your opportunity as the leader of the assembly to set high expectations of pupil behaviour and attitude cannot be over-emphasised. The pupils will model themselves on you. It is best to be yourself, sincere and authentic. Pupils are quick to spot inconsistencies in adult behaviour. They will avoid entering into the spirit of an assembly if they sense that your inner world is discordant. It will help if you are able to take a minute or two before the assembly to centre yourself so that you are as relaxed as possible. The crucial thing is to maintain an honest approach and avoid false piety.

"The pupils will model themselves on you."

The role of reflection and silence

Reflection, sometimes known as creative visualisation or stilling, is a teaching strategy that can be used in class as well as assembly (see Chapter 6). It helps pupils focus and value their positive aspects. It should be a key element in a values assembly. The length of time allowed for it can be increased as pupils become used to the technique.

Crucial elements of silent reflection

- The assembly leader uses appropriate words to stimulate the creation of pictures in the minds of the pupils.
- Pupils develop the skill to go within themselves, becoming observers of their thoughts in order to nurture positive images that support positive behaviour.
- It creates an appropriate atmosphere for reflection.
- It encourages pupils to sit in a relaxed, alert, comfortable and still manner.
- Pupils are trained to use the inner eye of imagination.

Here is an example of a reflection. You may like to think about the purpose behind each of its four parts.

> ① This morning in a moment of silence let us sit very still, close our eyes and feel relaxed.
> ② On the screen of your mind, see yourself in your classroom, working hard at an activity, co-operating with others. Feel good about this work.
> ③ Now think about our month's value – trust – and think about someone you really trust. How do we become trustworthy, so others will trust us? What qualities do we need to develop? Patience, tact, friendliness, co-operation and honesty may be some of the qualities.
> ④ Choose one to think about during the day. Now open your eyes again.

In step 1, the words, which are often used, invite pupils to adopt a particular physical and mental attitude to set the scene for the reflection. Pupils come to understand the expression 'on the screen of your mind' in step 2 and with practice learn to use their creative imagination. Positive feelings are invited about working with others in the classroom. In step 3 the month's value word *trust* is used. Thinking about someone the child trusts helps to develop a deeper understanding of the concept before turning to think about self-development. Finally, in step 4 pupils are invited to take the thinking developed during the reflection into the rest of the day. This helps in the development of the value by making it a recurring theme.

Planning

Planning is important. Last-minute thinking does not create meaningful assemblies. Your values assemblies can be based on a yearly plan that incorporates monthly values and weekly themes. It is important that all staff feel comfortable with the proposed values and themes. All should feel a sense of ownership of both the process and content of the assemblies.

The yearly plan opposite give examples of values and themes.

Yearly plan

Term 1	Value	Theme
Week 1	Quality	Values
Week 2		Religious ceremonies
Week 3		Prayer/reflection
Week 4	Unity	Famous people
Week 5		Health week (care for yourself)
Week 6		Aspects of Hinduism
Week 7		Harvest
Week 8	Peace	Remembrance
		Discussion about conflict – prayer for peace
Week 9		Jesus
Week 10		Feelings/thoughts
Week 11		Worship
Week 12	Happiness	Individual differences
Week 13		Positive attitudes/character/personality
Week 14		Christmas

Term 2	Value	Theme
Week 1	Hope	The Bible
Week 2		Beauty and wonder
Week 3	Patience	Places of worship, church, temple and other sacred, special or personal places
Week 4		Love – different sorts for different things
Week 5		Spring – new beginnings
Week 6	Care	Dying (loss)
Week 7		Mothers – their role, rest of the family Mother's day
Week 8		Excellence: examples from religious stories
Week 9		Easter
Week 10		Community Humility
Week 11		Celebrating the birth, death and enlightenment of the Buddha
Week 12		Birth of a child, growth, babies, new member of family, baptism

Term 3	Value	Theme
Week 1	Simplicity	Learning about drugs
Week 2		Friends of Jesus Relationships
Week 3		Environment – care
Week 4	Understanding	Disability, including blindness and deafness
Week 5	Trust	What are religious artefacts?
Week 6		Co-operation, kindness, doing your best, enjoyment
Week 7		People in need Charity
Week 8		Care of animals
Week 9	Freedom	Journeys
Week 10		Giving thanks

You will see that the value for Term 3, weeks 5 to 8, is *trust* and an assembly theme associated with this is 'Care of animals'. On page 42 there is a mind-map that was constructed as the planning tool for that assembly.

Themes for acts of worship and associated activities

In this section two more mind-maps for values-based assemblies are presented (see pages 43 and 44). On page 62 you will find a photocopiable outline to use when planning your own assemblies.

Assembly record sheet

GOOD PRACTICE PRIMARY SCHOOL
ACTS OF WORSHIP RECORD SHEET

VALUE: Trust
THEME: Care of animals

DATE: 26.6.2002

LEARNING INTENTION: All things in nature: plants/animals are interconnected and have their place in the world. Human beings must take responsibility for looking after the world and everything in it.

WORSHIP OUTLINE: (Begin with reflection and end with prayer. Incorporate a song/hymn where appropriate.)

Bible reading
Luke 15 v 1-7
Lost sheep shows the shepherd's love for the sheep and God's love for us

5

School's council awards/ announcements
Prayer (see below)

6

1

Music
(dolphin music)
Reflection

Care of animals

4

2

Why?
- responsibility
- NSPCA
- St Francis – patron saint
- if we don't, balance of nature upset

School song
- motto – care and excellence
- school symbol
- dolphin – why
- discuss with pupils

3

Story: A pet: show picture of Charlie – what sort of dog? (headteacher's dog)

Value: trust
- stray
- brought home – describe what he did: running away
- goes everywhere with us
- whole family love him

Ask children to be very still, silent
- bring Charlie into assembly
- talk about how we care for Charlie

REFLECTION: Let us sit very still and on the screen of our minds see our favourite animals. See them enjoying their lives. Think now how we should care for these animals . . .

PRAYER: Let us sit quite still and, closing our eyes, let us pray:

Dear God, thank you for our natural world with all its animals. We give thanks today for our pets. May we be ever mindful of our responsibility towards our pets, showing them care, consideration and kindness so that they can always trust us. Amen.

GROUP OF PUPILS: All

TEACHER: Neil

Assembly record sheet

GOOD PRACTICE PRIMARY SCHOOL
ASSEMBLY RECORD SHEET

VALUE: Simplicity
THEME: Drugs

DATE: 13.05.2002

LEARNING INTENTION: To think about the meaning of simplicity.

WORSHIP OUTLINE: (Begin with reflection and end with prayer. Incorporate a song/hymn where appropriate.)

Simplicity: Appreciating the simple things in life and nature; freedom from material desires and emotional desires – simply 'be'; avoids waste, teaches economy, avoids value clashes complicated by greed, fear, peer pressure and a false sense of identity; from it grows generosity, sharing; putting others first with kindness, openness, pure intentions without expectations and conditions.

Class activity
- sit or stand in a quiet spot on our field – look, listen, stay still for 5 minutes
- write a poem on your thoughts/feelings – could be a tree writing to you
- read your story out next Monday

Awareness of God's Earth – Genesis creation

Relationships that are uncomplicated
- develop friendships – discuss how
- time and patience needed to develop good relationships
- don't be critical – look for the good in others
- be interested in your friend – don't expect too much from them
- discuss: how can we keep relationships simple?

Simplicity

Drugs
- smoking – why? – children here don't but later do
- your body works best when it:
  – has rest
  – isn't stressed
  – has good food
  – isn't given harmful drugs

Learn from
The Earth:
– look, care, help to protect, don't ignore, time to look.
A trip on the canals
– quietness except for railway, animals, slow pace, colours.
Ask the children for examples.

What is simplicity?

- being natural
- appreciating the world
- appreciating beauty – sunset
- opposite of complicated
- staying in the present – don't worry about future and past
- enjoying being peaceful
- appreciating the small things in life

REFLECTION/PRAYER: Let us think about our beautiful world. You could be a secret world helper. When you are walking by yourself and enjoying nature, sometimes there is a chance to give a little back to Mother Earth: by picking up rubbish, by walking around a little flower that is starting to spring up from the soil, by gently helping an insect which is stuck in a pool of water. Dear God, thank you for our beautiful world. Help us to keep it beautiful. Amen.

GROUP OF PUPILS: All

TEACHER: John

Assembly record sheet

GOOD PRACTICE PRIMARY SCHOOL
ACTS OF WORSHIP RECORD SHEET

VALUE: Quality
THEME: Prayer/Reflection
DATE: 20.9.2002

LEARNING INTENTION: To understand the what, why and how of prayer and reflection.

WORSHIP OUTLINE: *(Begin with reflection and end with prayer. Incorporate a song/hymn where appropriate.)*

Prayer/reflection

P R A Y E R
See below

Activity for classwork (7)
- write a class prayer to use in class
- send copy to me/school's council to choose a school prayer to use in assemblies
- learn your class prayer by heart, also Lord's Prayer
(6)

Experience reflection and discuss (1)

Let us sit still, with straight backs, with our hands in our laps. With eyes closed be aware of your breathing. As you breathe feel relaxed and peaceful. Now, on the screen of your mind picture yourself doing something that makes you feel very happy. With this warm, good feeling gently open your eyes and bring your attention back to our assembly.

Link theme of the assembly to the value – quality (5)

PRAYER (2)
What do pupils know?
Prayer:
What? Talking to God.
Why? 1. Helps to make us better people.
How? 2. Saying thank you for our life and world (see below).

Benefits of reflection: (4)
- regulates heartbeat and breath > calm relaxes > reduces stress > good health
- lets you get to know yourself and to be in control (you are the 'driver' in your body)
- you're able to concentrate for longer and you don't get so upset
- improves memory and your intelligence
- gives a time when you think about your day (bedtime – early morning)

Reflection: thinking in a quiet setting (3)
Teacher explains the following elements:
1. sit comfortably with straight backs
2. be as still as you can
3. relax your body, shoulders etc.
4. close eyes and focus on thoughts
5. let mind relax
6. think good thoughts.
Discuss: many people find that reflection helps when praying.

REFLECTION: Today we have been thinking about prayer and the need to practise being still and quiet so that we can still our thoughts. That makes our prayers to God more meaningful. In a minute of silence, practise being still with eyes shut and say your own prayer to God.
PRAYER: Dear God, thank you for our school and the opportunities it gives us to learn about ourselves and your wonderful world. Amen.

GROUP OF PUPILS: Key Stage 2   **TEACHER:** John

The essential elements of a successful assembly

Remember

- Arrive early before the assembly begins to ensure that the room is properly prepared.
- Ensure that appropriate music is played as the pupils enter the hall.
- Make sure that the hall will support a good atmosphere. Check the quality of cleanliness, display, heating, ventilation and tidiness.
- Coloured spot lighting, if available, will help create a special warm atmosphere.
- Sit down and model the behaviour you expect of everyone coming to the assembly. A relaxed, friendly yet serious attitude works well. Avoid exaggerated smiles or gestures as they may act as a signal for inappropriate social interaction.
- Avoid looking on assembly as a time to entertain the pupils. The inexperienced visiting speaker sometimes falls into that trap. Poor behaviour and inappropriate responses often follow.

To ensure that your assembly achieves your aim of providing a quality experience, consider and talk with colleagues about the following important issues.

Issues

- You will need to model stillness as the children enter the hall.
- Members of staff should avoid talking to each other or acting to police the behaviour of the pupils. Such action creates a negative perception of what assembly is about.
- Use eye contact with as many pupils and staff as possible during the first few minutes. This demonstrates that each person is valued and respected. Sensitivity is necessary in employing this technique. Remember to explain to the pupils beforehand what eye contact is for and why it is used. Eye contact demonstrates that connections can be established between people without exaggerated gesture. It is a highly effective way of establishing discipline, as each pupil becomes aware that they are being actively observed.
- You will maintain control in subtle ways, such as through your self-confidence. A held look to a pupil who is not focused is usually all that is needed to check inappropriate behaviour.

Ensure that the assembly has an enriching quality by associating the theme with the experience of the pupils. This makes the experience relevant and real to them. Telling an inspiring story, such as 'The Selfish Giant' by Oscar Wilde, will enable pupils to make connections with their own attitudes and behaviour. Relating your own personal experience to the theme of the assembly and drawing in other members of staff to comment can be enriching. Relating exciting experiences, such as being taken on the back of a motorbike dressed in appropriate kit, grabs the full attention of everyone. Describing the journey with all its thoughts, feelings and emotions enables you to illustrate a theme that relates to real experiences. Such communication technique helps to connect

"Today's assembly is on simplicity."

the subject matter with the pupils' own lives. Teachers will enjoy the assembly too if they feel that they are being spiritually nourished.

Connections are needed if pupils are to grasp the relevance to them of the values and principles discussed during assembly. We want them to say 'Yes, I'll try that, I'll change today!' Guidance and encouragement are prerequisites for enabling pupils to have that inner debate that eventually modifies their behaviour through self-regulation and self-discipline.

You may also help to reinforce the concept of the school as a community by giving appropriate praise. Referring to positive examples of good behaviour or work creates a culture of success and high pupil self-esteem.

Finally, remember to involve and maintain pupil interest by changing the tone of your voice and your physical position.

The prayer or reflection at the end should encapsulate the learning objective of the assembly. It need not be long. Spend some time working out appropriate wording. An example is 'Help us to make our love unconditional and give to others often.' (The story used in the assembly would have explained the meaning of 'unconditional'.)

'Referring to positive examples of good behaviour or work creates a culture of success and high pupil self-esteem.'

Children's assemblies

Pupils should be encouraged to present a values assembly. The following assembly was the final stage of teaching, learning and understanding about hope. These are some of the activities that the Year 5 pupils, led by their teacher Linda, experienced on the theme of hope during one month.

- ❍ An assembly that introduced the value of hope, led by the headteacher.
- ❍ A specific lesson on hope by the class teacher.
- ❍ Implicit teaching about hope across all curriculum time (i.e. in all lessons).
- ❍ Modelling the value by the class teacher.
- ❍ Parents receiving information about how to support the school's teaching about hope.
- ❍ The creation of an assembly about hope led by the pupils.

The assembly

The assembly began with a pupil welcoming the children and inviting them to join in the singing of 'Peace is flowing like a river'. (The song includes the words 'Hope is flowing like a river . . . setting all the people free.')

The pupils then talked about the value of hope and what they had been thinking about it. They had thought about their personal hopes for the year, their hopes for their families and their hopes for the world around them. (This section is a synthesis of the lesson about hope.)

The children then introduced the story of Pandora's box, saying that hope is more than wishes. They told the story in a short drama culminating in their showing what dreadful things were let out of Pandora's box when she opened it. The one thing that remained in the box was hope; hope would help the world cope with all the dreadful things. They explained that hope is something we need when life gets difficult for us.

The action shifted to a scene in the playground. Children were playing hockey. A boy was being criticised by his classmates for not doing well. He explained that it was not his fault; he had had an operation on his leg – he felt that it was hopeless for him to do well at the game. We were invited by a narrator to think about times that seemed hopeless and to remember that we should keep our hopes alive. We should think well of ourselves, telling ourselves that we are good enough. We can also rely on others to help us – our friends and family.

'We should think well of ourselves, telling ourselves that we are good enough.'

A pupil explained the main learning points of the assembly, written on a whiteboard in the hall:
① Remember that you have got through difficult times before.
② Remember that you are good enough as a person.
③ Rely on others around you to help.

We were told that hope is a strength that we feel inside ourselves – we should remember that.

A pupil came to the front and set the scene for a prayer. He said:
Dear God, let us remember to stay hopeful. You have made each of us the special person we are. Difficult times come and go in our lives. We call on hope to see us through. Amen.

The headteacher then thanked the children for an excellent assembly and talked to them about his experience with the value of hope. Practical examples were used to reinforce the learning points of the assembly.

The pupils who were members of the school's council then gave out certificates to children who had been living the school's values.

The assembly ended with the headteacher saying that during the following month we would be thinking about a new value, the value of patience.

This chapter describes how you can transform an assembly into an activity that becomes central to the life of the school. Outstanding values assemblies occur when you make a positive connection between you and those taking part. The skill of reflection, a vital part of values assemblies and other aspects of the curriculum, is the subject of the next chapter.

Chapter 6
The role of reflection and silent sitting

*I think about other people a lot more than I used to since we learnt about values.
I think about people's feelings and how they would feel if I was horrible to them.
How I would feel if they said it to me.*

Amanda, Year 6

The importance of stillness and reflection

During the past few years a number of teachers have been developing an effective teaching technique known as *reflection* or *silent sitting*. They have found that through using it their teaching has become both more effective and enjoyable. Karen Errington has carefully developed reflection as a key aspect of her teaching, and I am delighted to draw on her practical experience in this chapter. I recognise that you may be using the technique already, particularly during assembly. What follows will help both those who want to get started and those who want to refine and develop their practice.

A period of silence at the beginning of a lesson followed by a simple reflection, during which the children are asked to consider the work that they are about to do or have completed, is an excellent technique to develop positive thinking skills. The use of reflection develops the imaginative side of the brain, which promotes creativity and problem-solving. You will find that periods of stillness help to create a learning-centred atmosphere that gives each child the opportunity to achieve success. The classroom's quiet and reflective atmosphere is not something that is imposed but that grows out of the expectations and behaviour of the teacher. A reflective atmosphere can be promoted, especially in more challenging classrooms, by using appropriate music that helps to develop a peaceful atmosphere during working periods. Once we are clear in our own minds about the aim of a reflection – to relax, calm and still; to focus the mind, create some mental space and get in touch with our inner selves – it is of prime importance to become aware that we as teachers are the primary participant and role model for the pupils. If they are to achieve stillness and calm the teacher must achieve that first. If they are to be focused, the teacher must be totally focused too.

Key skills

Using reflection promotes an atmosphere that raises achievement and encourages quality in all aspect of schoolwork. In order to be effective, the teacher needs to be self-reflective and confident. They should model what they expect of their pupils. Being real and accepting that none of us is perfect is important. Show that you are a good listener too. This helps the pupils understand that you respect them and want to develop good relationships with each of them. Socratic questioning – using questioning to enable pupils to develop their thinking – is another key teaching skill; it bridges the gap between what a pupil needs to know and what they understand.

In the following account Karen Errington shares her experience of teaching reflection at Windmill First School in Oxford. You will find her experience very compelling and will want to have a go yourself if it is new to you. Remember to start with yourself; the calmer and more reflective you are, the more your pupils will be too.

Case study: Karen's experience in teaching reflection

I have no doubt that my effectiveness as a teacher has been greatly enhanced because I have introduced my pupils to periods of quiet reflection. I demand high standards from the pupils and myself and I have found that the techniques that I talk about here have been central to achieving them. In this article written for you, the teacher, I have outlined:

- Some of the reasons why I continue to make time for reflection within the school day.
- Year 4 pupils' responses to reflection times.
- Suggestions for introducing pupils to the reflection process.
- Some tips to ensure your success.

Do you recognise this scene?
Sam and Eric, having just had a go at each other in the playground, were escorted into class by the senior lunchtime supervisor. Another child, Suzy, was standing next to me sobbing because, she said, everyone hated her. Initially the afternoon did not look promising.

Emotions were spiralling out of control and I needed to restore calm and a sense of purpose. If I failed in this I knew that the afternoon would be neither productive nor pleasant. At this point I asked the pupils to sit, either close their eyes or focus on a spot on the floor, and be very still. I quietly explained that I wanted to give everyone the opportunity to calm down and make the right choices, as I felt some children were about to make choices that might make them feel miserable. Within minutes, the atmosphere of the class had changed from one of tension and diversity to one of calm and unity.

I led the class in a reflection, creating through my words a positive, calm atmosphere in the room. Between pauses I posed questions for the children: 'Think of a pleasant moment at playtime – either from today or last week. Why did it feel good? What did you do to make it enjoyable? Was today's play as good? Why? If not, how could you have acted differently?'

I finished the reflection on a positive note, asking the pupils to feel the joy of love, of friendship from another child, parent or adult. After a concluding moment of stillness the children opened their eyes – now more relaxed, focused and in control of their emotions, and ready to concentrate on their afternoon lessons.

This process took two to three minutes and had a dramatic impact upon the class. This quiet time offered the children a chance to enter their inner worlds and to explore their actions and feelings. Without the external pressure of others judging them, they are more likely to be honest with themselves. This 'time out' gives the children an opportunity to learn about themselves, gain control over their emotions and refocus their thoughts in a positive way.

The use of reflection has made my role as a teacher easier. However, I should make it clear at this point that my class has worked hard to develop the skill of reflection – it needs to be built up slowly. It is a technique worth developing.

Case study

Case study

Case study: Karen's experience in teaching reflection continued

I also use silent sitting to enable pupils to become more involved in a lesson. For example, before leading a discussion on caring for animals I asked each child to sit still, close their eyes and 'see' their favourite animal being happy . . . eating . . . moving freely . . . and then to consider what made it unique. The children then opened their eyes and listened to a story about an adult mistreating a wild animal. When the story finished I asked each child to consider why the adult hurt the animal. Did they not realise that animals feel pain, and can enjoy life?

Often during class discussions pupils are expected to make instant responses with little thinking time allowed. Careful delivery of questions, giving the pupils space and time to reach deeper answers, is an important feature of reflection.

Time for reflection can encourage the development of the pupils' awareness of themselves and others, and of the role they play in making positive relationships. For example, after a story about two giants losing their tempers I asked the pupils to reflect on whether the giants' actions were justified. I then extended their thinking by asking the pupils to consider a time when they lost their temper and think about whether their actions were reasonable and helped the situation.

Reflection times also provide an excellent forum for raising pupils' self-esteem and helping them to recognise positive attributes in each other. I praise and thank the class for their enthusiasm and efforts and make anonymous references to pupils, praising and thanking them too. Whilst doing this, fleeting smiles cross faces and I perhaps receive the odd look. Reflection time enables me to focus on and acknowledge class and individual efforts.

I also use reflection to focus the pupils' minds on key learning objectives, either at the start or end of a lesson. When the pupils feel relaxed and calm, they are more likely to concentrate on the lesson and be open to learning.

Lastly, I believe reflection is beneficial for its own sake. During each day pupils and adults are bombarded with thousands of messages from the outside and thousands of their own thoughts from the inside. We are told a healthy lifestyle is all about balance, and yet in our busy lives there is little to redress the fast pace and potentially high stress levels that we face. I believe a few minutes' silent sitting help to restore peace and balance all our lives. This process reinforces my view that true happiness comes from within and is not synonymous with buying entertainment.

Periods of reflection enable me to return to the fundamental reason I became an educator, that of making a difference to someone's life, and to the education of character.

I highly recommend it – for both your pupils and yourself.

Introducing pupils to reflection

Explain carefully

Here is Karen's checklist to guide you in the technique of using reflection with your class or in your school.

① *What will happen?* Tell pupils reflection will involve the following:
  - One to two minutes of listening and paying attention to their thoughts and feelings. Sitting still and relaxed. (Acknowledge that reflection is challenging and needs practice.)
② *What do you expect from pupils?* Tell pupils you want them to:
  - privately consider the questions or statements posed;
  - be honest and open with themselves – they won't be made to share their reflection thoughts;

- take this activity seriously and, if they are finding it difficult, not disturb anyone else.

③ *Why reflection is worth doing*
- It makes explicit the link between a pupil's state of mind and mental/physical performance.
- It makes explicit the link between self-discipline and enhanced achievement (e.g. footballers, athletes, actors, politicians).
- Silent sitting enables individuals to quieten their mind and body and be peaceful. In this state individuals can more effectively consider issues and develop their inner thoughts.

④ *How to sit*
- Ask children to face you, with back and head straight but relaxed (do not place children facing each other).
- Explain that holding your left hand in your right hand and placing both in your lap helps still the whole body.
- Ask pupils to close their eyes or focus on a spot on the floor.
- Tell pupils you will watch and see how well they manage the reflection. (Explain that when they have mastered the art of reflection you will participate too.)

⑤ *Answer pupil questions.* Ask pupils if there are any questions. In the early stages these may include the following:
- What do I do if I can't concentrate? (Remember to sit still and practice breathing in a regular, quiet way – it is best to demonstrate what you mean.)
- Will I go to sleep? (No, because you will be listening and being aware of your thoughts and feelings.)
- I think I may laugh, what should I do? (It may seem strange at first, but you will find that everyone joining in will help you to stay focused.) [What to do when children laugh during a reflection is explained in the section on troubleshooting.]
- What is 'being focused'? (Concentrate on the centre of your forehead; this fixes your concentration. Being able to concentrate is being focused.)

When questions are answered begin your reflection.

"I feel like a peaceful river."

What Karen's Year 4 pupils say about reflection times

- It is a time to be calm and relaxed.
- It gives your brain time to think and you don't have everyone butting in all the time.
- I feel like a peaceful river.
- It's a time for you.
- I felt silly to start with but now I'm used to it. I like it, I don't know why!

Troubleshooting

- If some pupils laugh, calmly and quietly ask all the pupils to open their eyes and enquire 'Why do you think some people are finding this difficult?'

'Teachers have found that through silent reflection children learn to be more confident in articulating their views.'

Acknowledge that it may seem strange sitting as they are, and explain that it will become easier with practice. Invite those pupils to try again or sit out. (Karen has only ever had one pupil sit out, and he joined in again soon.) It is, of course, important that the work of the class is set in the context of rules that you and the class have formulated together. These rules, positively framed, will make it clear that mutual respect is important for the wellbeing of the class. Try having rules for the teacher too – children really appreciate it. Inappropriate behaviour is less likely to occur when these agreed rules operate. Teachers find that the more the values approach is adopted in a school, the less need there is for sanctions. Any sanctions that are used should be consistent and seen to be fair.

○ Start with short reflections (1 minute) and gradually build up to longer sessions (5 minutes).

○ With challenging classes stickers could be given to several individuals for effort and involvement in reflection.

○ Create the right atmosphere – dimming classroom lights and lighting a candle may help make reflection time feel special. Music can also help to create a calm and reflective mood. Music shops now sell a variety of appropriate relaxation music. Here is a word of warning: listen to the music first to make sure it is suitable.

○ You as teacher need to model how to sit and to show you take the activity seriously through your tone of voice and good planning. Never attempt to do anything during a reflection other than model the behaviour you require.

Remember to acknowledge the pupils

At the close of a session try dismissing pupils individually and in silence with a very subtle eye movement. This encourages pupils to have direct eye contact with you and ensures you acknowledge each child.

The positive effect of reflection – developing responsibility for learning

As you can see from Karen's example, reflection aids the development of good relationships between pupils and between adults and pupils. Above all, it sets the climate for pupils to be self-disciplined and to take responsibility for their learning. Your task is to focus on developing an attitude of mind in the pupil that encourages them. Pupils need positive affirmation, as do staff. The ideal atmosphere in the classroom supports the principle that teacher and pupil are joint partners in the learning process. This attitude creates a feeling of mutual respect and a relationship of working together. Teachers have found that through silent reflection children learn to be more confident in articulating their views. They learn how to express themselves assertively and respectfully.

Teachers have found that they are at their most effective when they are giving pupils appropriate questions to consider that extend their thinking. Sufficient time to reflect on the teacher's questions before being required to answer is very important in discursive lessons. If it is not given, the pupil searches for a quick answer that will satisfy the teacher. If the answer is incorrect, then the teacher is likely to ask another, more simple question and so on, until the pupil answers a question correctly. This practice is of limited value in helping the pupil to develop appropriate reflective thinking skills.

Karen drew our attention to asking the children to sit correctly. I mention this on page 24, but it is worth emphasising. Research teaches us that the general mental and physical health of children (and adults) is enhanced if they are encouraged to sit correctly. Reflection gives them time to practise the correct sitting position. It is one of the main reasons why reflection leads to increased concentration; children learn to control their bodies in a comfortable position that enhances the quality of breathing.

Examples of reflections for you to try

Here are three reflections to help you to get started. The first is one that I have used with children who have just been introduced to reflection. The other two I have used with children who are used to the practice.

The first reflection was used when I was talking with a group of children about their summer holidays, two weeks before the end of term.

> I want you to sit with straight backs, with your hands resting gently in your laps. Close your eyes. Keeping your body quite still, keeping your eyes closed, just think about your breathing. As you breathe in, breathe in a feeling of happiness; and as you breathe out, breathe out any feelings or thoughts that might be making you feel unhappy. (Pause) Now, think about a television screen and see yourself on it, enjoying a summer holiday, free from any cares or worries . . . , see yourself doing things that you really enjoy . . . , perhaps you are with other people . . . , just think about that for a few moments . . . Now get yourself ready to open your eyes and be aware of our room and today . . . . Open your eyes.

The reflection above will stimulate discussion and give opportunities to develop oracy.

The next reflection was used at an assembly at which the value was courage and the theme was members of the family at home and the family of the school.

> Let us be still and think. Close your eyes and, as you listen to the music (quiet, calming music playing in the background), imagine your family . . . see them all in turn. Feel good about them. See yourself helping a member of your family. See that person being pleased with you. Enjoy the feeling that this brings . . . , a feeling of happiness. Now see someone on the screen of your mind who is a part of the family of the school . . . Is this person someone you care about? Think how you show your care. See yourself helping this person and making them smile . . . Think about what you could do today in the classroom – without anyone knowing – that would show that you care about someone who perhaps is not one of your closest friends . . . Think about that for a few moments . . .

The last example is a longer reflection that I have used with Year 6 pupils who are experienced in the use of reflection. You could adapt the language to make it suitable for younger pupils. Following this reflection we had a discussion about their qualities and how we often focus too much on qualities that we think we haven't got. Such discussions help to develop self-worth.

> Sit still and comfortably, feeling alert but relaxed . . . On the screen of your mind see yourself in a beautiful field. It has been raining but now there is a rainbow in the sky, brilliant against the backdrop of a deep blue sky. You feel happy and peaceful as you walk across the field towards a wood. There is a little wooden gate at the entrance of the wood, with creaking hinges. You enter the wood and are aware of the range of delightful smells that the plants and trees give off as they dry in the warm sunlight. You follow a path which meanders through the tall trees to a clearing, at the centre of which is your friend, who welcomes you with open arms. You feel so relaxed in this person's company and are able to open your heart's desires. Your friend has a box made of beautifully carved wood on which is written 'Your qualities'. You open the box and see four coloured stones. On each is written one of your qualities. You pick them up, studying each in turn, feeling that quality within . . . Your friend says that it is time for you to take your present and return home. With joy in your heart, you say goodbye to your friend and, retracing your steps, return through the gate to your field. You stand quietly for a few moments . . . Now come back to this room and gently open your eyes.

Key reasons for using reflection

Why am I encouraging you to use reflection? Reflection gives the pupil time to be peaceful and to practise being aware of their thoughts, and through this awareness they become able to control their emotional responses and act appropriately.

Here are some other reasons for using reflection:

- ● Reflection helps to create balance in pupils' lives.
- ● It is an opportunity to focus the pupils, and calm them ready for a lesson.
- ● It gives pupils a technique that will help them to be calm and focused throughout the lesson.
- ● It is a time to enhance pupils' self-esteem and self-discipline and help them to feel positive about each other.
- ● It is an opportunity to consider the targets and skills that will be used in the lesson – to set the scene for it.
- ● It encourages pupils to spend time with their thoughts and acknowledge the strengths they have.
- ● It develops pupils' emotional intelligence and thereby raises achievement and standards.
- ● It increases their personal involvement in lessons by developing empathy and by jointly exploring ideas.
- ● It gives opportunities to reflect deeply whilst searching for more meaningful answers.
- ● It encourages self-awareness and understanding of others.
- ● It provides a meaningful opportunity to focus on the main learning objectives, either at the start or end of a lesson.
- ● If used as a closing activity, it encourages recognition of the learning that has taken place.
- ● It gives the teacher peace of mind in the knowledge that the whole child is being developed and educated (i.e. body, mind and spirit).
- ● It returns the joy to teaching because that becomes easier as the pupils become more internally motivated.

'Reflection gives the pupil time to be peaceful and to practise being aware of their thoughts.'

Finally, I should like another teacher to have the last word on this subject:

Well certainly, I think the children's concentration becomes greater. I think the children have very good concentration and thought processes. The teaching about values improves the concentration because it makes the children comfortable with themselves.

Craig McConnell, Year 3 teacher

Chapter 7
Values education policy and resources

I think values education is good because it helps you to build relationships. It makes you feel safe and secure – it's hard to explain. It's a warm feeling, like drinking happy juice or something. You have a quick swig of it and you instantly feel happy. It helps you not to worry about little things like whose ruler it is but the things that are important.

Gareth, Year 5

'Remember that you are values education's greatest and most effective resource.'

This final chapter will give you some practical help as you introduce values education. Before you move on to it, complete your own personal action plan (see page 63). It is in two sections: the first is about developing values in yourself, the second about implementing the values in your classroom. Do complete this as soon as possible. Teachers tell me that it has helped them to be clear about what they are going to do. It also acts as an *aide-mémoire*.

This chapter is divided into two parts. First, it offers you a model school policy for values education. Please adapt it to suit the context of your school. The rationale section is based on the policy statement adopted at Stonesfield School in Oxfordshire (see page 10). Secondly, there is a list of useful resources. Remember that you are values education's greatest and most effective resource.

Values education policy

Aim
To raise standards by promoting a school ethos which is underpinned by core values that support the development of the whole child as a reflective learner.

Rationale
At our school we are giving a great deal of thought to the values that we are trying to promote. We regularly consider our core values and how the school sustains an ethos which supports the pupil as a reflective learner and promotes quality teaching and learning. We are very much aware that society is faced with enormously complicated problems which make growing up a difficult process. Children are constantly bombarded with negative messages that adversely affect their mental, emotional and spiritual development. Also, they are repeatedly being given the impression that happiness is totally obtainable from a material world. They are conditioned to believe that 'things' will provide happiness. For example, advertisements encourage children to believe that the only source of entertainment is television or videos. Children are generally encouraged to experience life in a world totally external to their inner selves: a world which is full of noise and constant activity. Impressions of society being violent and selfish leave their mark as the child develops into adolescence.

Symptoms of pupil stress are revealed when children find it difficult to listen attentively and to give schoolwork their full concentration. Social relationships suffer as the child often fails to appreciate that building meaningful relationships is their responsibility.

As a school community, we believe the ethos of the school should be built on a foundation of core values such as *honesty, respect, happiness, responsibility, tolerance* and *peace*. These will at times be addressed directly through lessons and the acts of worship programme, but they will permeate the whole curriculum. They are the basis for the social, intellectual, emotional, spiritual and moral development of the child. We encourage pupils to consider these values, thereby developing knowledge, skills and attitudes that enable them to develop as reflective learners and grow to be stable, educated and civilised adults.

Elements of teaching and learning

The elements of values education are as follows:

- Ensuring that the school's institutional values are consistent with the values that pupils are encouraged to develop.
- Actively promoting a whole-school policy that has the support of all staff and is led and monitored by the headteacher.
- A programme of school assemblies that introduce monthly values. Pupils are also encouraged to be involved in exploring their understanding of values in pupil-led assemblies.
- By direct teaching about values in values lessons. These lessons provide opportunities for personal reflection and moral discourse, and include an appropriate activity to promote understanding. Teaching and learning about values takes place in the following steps:
  ① Teachers explaining the meaning of a value.
  ② Pupils reflecting on the value and relating it to their own behaviour.
  ③ Pupils using the value to guide their own actions.
- Staff modeling the values through their own behaviour.
- Ensuring that values are taught implicitly through every aspect of the curriculum.

Values lessons

A few thoughts about values lessons may be helpful.

Classroom ethos – Maintaining an ethos in the classroom that is positive and all-inclusive, with an atmosphere of equality, will help children gain most from values lessons. It is important that any approach to class management is in line with the values being taught. Children soon feel secure and able to share their thoughts, feelings and experiences when they know that these are always welcomed and valued. Children will respond quickly when the teacher is aware that they are an important role model.

Reflection (stilling/silent sitting) – Most of the lessons would begin with a period of reflection. This is explained in Chapter 6.

'Maintaining an ethos in the classroom that is positive and all-inclusive, with an atmosphere of equality, will help children gain most from values lessons.'

'Values education is the way to help our young people to grow into well-balanced individuals who can contribute positively to society.'

Story-telling – Using a story where possible as a stimulus for the lesson has many advantages. It can put across the value in a way that all levels of awareness can access. It generates feelings, captures attention and often inspires. The listener is able to find parallels in their own experiences, which can help in future difficult situations.

Lesson format – Every lesson should have a section on teacher understanding, in which the teacher 'translates' their understanding into the living experience of the child. Next is a stimulus for the lesson that may be based on a story, discussion, experience, artifact and so on. This is followed by the teacher-led discussion that lies at the core of the lesson. The lessons are not theoretical, but aim to help pupils to modify and expand their own thoughts and actions. Finally, an activity is included to encourage pupils to engage with the value, followed by a review to evaluate understanding.

Discussion – After the stimulus has been given and the learning objective has been made clear, whole-class discussion allows the value to be explored more deeply. The children gain insight from each other, especially if the teacher becomes practised in facilitating Socratic discussion, summarising ideas and leading the children into considering further possibilities. Use your own and the children's experiences as a basis for discussion, helping the children to close the gap between the value as an ideal and their expression of it.

Enjoyment – Children soon begin to look forward to their values lessons. They will know what to expect and will participate in all the elements with enthusiasm. As you learn to use the lessons you will develop your own ideas and activities. Teaching values across the curriculum then becomes automatic. Aim to make enjoyment a key element and you will see positive effects in many other areas of school life.

Conclusion

Now that you have read this book, I do hope that you will be inspired to put its ideas into practice. I am convinced that in the next few years we shall see teachers being asked to work with a curriculum that is more appropriately balanced between the cognitive and the affective domains. I'm equally convinced that values education is the way to help our young people to grow into well-balanced individuals who can contribute positively to society.

Resources

The following books and materials are very useful.

Don't Just Do Something, Sit There by Mary K. Stone. RMEP (1997). ISBN 1 85175 105 X

Education in Human Values. Manual and lesson plans. Contact June Auton, Lower Walbridge Farmhouse, Dowlish Wake, Ilminster, Somerset TA19 ONZ

Living Values. An international educational programme in values education. Visit www.hci-online.com and www.livingvalues.net for details

A Quiet Revolution by Frances Farrer. The story of the development of values education at West Kidlington Primary School in Oxfordshire. Rider (2000). ISBN 0 71260 577 0

Showing another Way by David Downton and Mike Sandy. Morleys Publishing. ISBN 0 86071 392 X

Turn your School Round by Jenny Mosley. LDA (1993). ISBN 1 85503 174 4

Values and Visions by Sally Burns and George & Anne Lamont. Hodder & Stoughton (1996). ISBN 0 340 64412 5

Invitation to parents

Dear Parent,

I'm delighted to have this opportunity of inviting you to a workshop as part of our class values education programme. As you know from our newsletters, we are helping the children to understand a range of basic values such as respect, co-operation, care, honesty and love. I know from the comments which many of you have made that you are pleased that the children are thinking about how to put these values into their lives. I am convinced that they will help your child get the most out of every aspect of school life.

I am keen to share the work that we are doing with you in a workshop. I should like to invite you to school on . . . . at . . . . Refreshments will be provided, and I promise that as well as being informed about our programme you will have a really enjoyable time. So that I know how many parents to expect, I should be grateful if you would return the enclosed form by . . . .

Yours sincerely,

. . . .

Values education programme

Workshop on . . . .   Name of your child . . . .

Please tick (a) or (b)
(a) I/We shall be attending the workshop.   (b) I/We shall not be attending the workshop.

Your name(s) . . . .

Please ask your child to return this form to their class teacher by . . . .

Dear Parent,

I'm delighted to have this opportunity of inviting you to a workshop as part of our class values education programme. As you know from our newsletters, we are helping the children to understand a range of basic values such as respect, co-operation, care, honesty and love. I know from the comments which many of you have made that you are pleased that the children are thinking about how to put these values into their lives. I am convinced that they will help your child get the most out of every aspect of school life.

I am keen to share the work that we are doing with you in a workshop. I should like to invite you to school on . . . . at . . . . Refreshments will be provided, and I promise that as well as being informed about our programme you will have a really enjoyable time. So that I know how many parents to expect, I should be grateful if you would return the enclosed form by . . . .

Yours sincerely,

. . . .

Values education programme

Workshop on . . . .   Name of your child . . . .

Please tick (a) or (b)
(a) I/We shall be attending the workshop.   (b) I/We shall not be attending the workshop.

Your name(s) . . . .

Please ask your child to return this form to their class teacher by . . . .

Planning sheet for values lesson

VALUE: . . . .   CLASS: . . . .

MONTH: . . . .

Teacher understanding

Reflection (what personal thoughts do you want to give the pupils time to consider?)

Stimulus (story, personal recount, reflection, quote, news headline)

Discussion (list key questions that will guide debate)

Activity (role play, artwork, poem, story, personal challenge)

Assembly record sheet

ASSEMBLY RECORD SHEET

VALUE/THEME: . . . .

LEARNING INTENTIONS: . . . .   DATE: . . . .

WORSHIP OUTLINE:

REFLECTION/PRAYER:

GROUP OF PUPILS: . . . .   TEACHER: . . . .

Action plan

Action Plan	Aim: What I intend to do	How I will achieve my aim	What are the likely obstacles?	How will I overcome the obstacles?	When I aim to do things
Working on the values in myself					
Implementing values education in my classroom					